The Buddhism
A Series of Introductory Articles

Compiled by
Jim Cowan

Published by NSUK

First published in 1982 by
Nichiren Shoshu of the United Kingdom
1 The Green, Richmond,
Surrey TW9 1PL

Copyright ©Nichiren Shoshu of the United
Kingdom, 1982
Second Reprint 1984
Third Reprint 1987
Fourth Reprint 1990

The title is available in paperback only. The paperback edition is sold subject to the condition that it shall not, by ways of trade or otherwise, be lent, re-sold, hired out or otherwise circulated in any form of binding or cover other than that in which it is published, and without a similar condition, including this condition, being imposed on the subsequent purchaser

All rights reserved

British Library Cataloguing in Publication Data
The Buddhism of the Sun.
1. Sōka Gakkai (Nichiren Shōshū)
I. Cowan, Jim
294.3   BQ8420
ISBN 0 9508274 0 1

Typeset, printed and bound in the UK by
Pindar Print London
Set in Garamond 3

Cover design, Errol Le Cain.
Book design and artwork,
Geoff Mack and Anna Donovan

Contents

Foreword 5
Introduction 6
A brief historical sketch 8

Part 1, The Buddhist View of Life
Poem Song of youth *Daisaku Ikeda* 11
Nine consciousnesses *Edward Clark and Chris Roman* 12
Cause and effect *Daisaku Ikeda* 19
Transforming the dark side of life *Yasuji Kirimura* 22
How people affect their environment *Barbara Cahill and Dick Causton* 25
The fusion of reality and wisdom *Sue Thornton* 28
Ten states everyone experiences *Barbara Cahill* 30
Revealing Buddhahood *Barbara Cahill* 35
Three thousand worlds in a moment of life *Pat Allwright and Jim Cowan* 38
What happens when we die? *Akemi Baynes* 42
Pursuit of the great middle way *Daisaku Ikeda* 46

Part 2, The Power of Practice
Poem Theme *Daisaku Ikeda* 50
'On Attaining Buddhahood' *Nichiren Daishonin* 51
The meaning of Nam-myoho-renge-kyo *Pat Allwright* 54
The power of Nam-myoho-renge-kyo *Takehisa Tsuji* 57
The Gohonzon: Life in the Buddha state *James Perry* 59
The Gohonzon: An in-depth explanation *Dick Causton* 62
On prayer *Daisaku Ikeda* 70
Changing karma *Akemi Baynes* 73
Daily practice: Gongyo *Dick Causton* 76

Part 3, Origins and Evolution
Poem Springing from the earth *Daisaku Ikeda* 80
Cosmos, religion, culture *Daisaku Ikeda* 81
The heritage of the Law *Dick Causton* 90
The growth of Nichiren Shoshu Buddhism *Mike Eggleton* 97
Working for peace *Jim Cowan* 100
Peace must prevail for mankind *Daisaku Ikeda* 105

Part 4, In Conclusion
Faith, practice and study 108
The true entity of life: A lecture *Daisaku Ikeda* 109

A profile of Daisaku Ikeda 118
Glossary 119
Sources 123
Other books 125

Foreword

Mostly due to our history of empire, libraries and museums in Britain contain a wealth of books and material on Hinayana (also known as Theravada) Buddhism. This is, generally speaking, the Buddhism of India, Sri Lanka and South East Asia. There is far less understanding in the UK of that other great flow of Buddhist teachings known as Mahayana, which, over hundreds of years, surged north and north east from India, through China to Korea and Japan. Of course there are exceptions. In particular, Tibetan Buddhism and the teachings of the Zen sect of Japan have had considerable publicity in the West in recent times. Nevertheless, a greater understanding of the significance of the Mahayana teachings is lacking especially in regard to their orientation towards the daily life of ordinary people, as compared to the tendency towards monasticism in Hinayana Buddhism.

This applies nowhere more particularly than in the case of the teachings of Nichiren Daishonin (1222-1282 AD), preserved down through the centuries in their original purity by Nichiren Shoshu, the orthodox school of Nichiren's Buddhism in Japan. Yet these true Mahayana teachings are today the source and the prime point of a world-wide Buddhist movement for peace and happiness involving millions of lay members in Japan and more than ninety other countries.

We are indebted to Jim Cowan for the time and energy he and a team of his fellow members of NSUK (Nichiren Shoshu of the United Kingdom) have devoted to compiling this book about the teachings and practice of Nichiren Daishonin's Buddhism – 'The Buddhism of the Sun'. It is this Buddhism which is designated specifically for this turbulent age; for ordinary people who wish to find the great middle way of balance and happiness, despite the inevitable pressures and anxieties of our times.

I wish also to express our gratitude to Mr Tomohiro Matsuda, a vice-chief of the study department of the Soka Gakkai, for his warm encouragement and advice on the preparation of this book from beginning to end.

Richard Causton
Chairman
Nichiren Shoshu of the United Kingdom (NSUK)

Introduction

As far as recorded history is concerned, Buddhism has existed for about 3,000 years and during that time has taken many forms. This book is called *The Buddhism of the Sun* because it is about the Buddhism of Nichiren Daishonin, which was established 700 years ago in Japan. The image of the sun indicates the essential Law or principles which are fundamental to all life and which are eternal. In the West what most people associate with the word Buddhism is pre-Nichiren Daishonin. Immediately following this introduction there is therefore a brief historical sketch which outlines how Buddhism has developed and indicating briefly why the Buddhism of Nichiren Daishonin is so important today.

Throughout its history the intent of Buddhist teachings has been to enable human beings to reveal the essential Law in their own lives. A Buddha is an enlightened person; someone who is enlightened to the essence of life, who is perfectly in harmony with the universal rhythm, and who deeply understands the eternity of life. Although the enlightened state is very special it is in no way superhuman. Buddhist teachings exist to lead people to their own enlightenment.

A major theme running through this book is how Nichiren Daishonin's Buddhism enables everyone to overcome what might loosely be called 'the darker side of life'. The Japanese have a much more precise word for this, *bon'no*, which has no exact equivalent in English. *Bon'no* are what we would call in English negative impulses, delusions or ignorance arising from our desires. It is important to appreciate that these are the negative aspects of our own lives operating at a deeper level than the conscious mind. They cannot be changed solely by training in positive thought.

Our inherent negativity can therefore be likened to any climatic condition which obscures the sun. The significance behind the title is that Nichiren Daishonin's Buddhism enables all human beings to transform the negative aspects of their lives into enlightenment: whether there be clouds, rain or fog the sun can always be revealed.

The reader should be clear that this is an introductory book to Nichiren Daishonin's Buddhism. Parts one and two are about the philosophy and practice. Part three explains how Buddhism has evolved, how Nichiren Daishonin's Buddhism has spread since the second world war, and how it has now become a worldwide movement for the establishment of peace. The Buddhism of Nichiren Daishonin is also referred to as Nichiren Shoshu, meaning 'Orthodox School of Nichiren's Buddhism'. It is a life-philosophy and practice which teaches the highest respect for life. Nichiren Shoshu is concerned with the condition of people's lives, the root cause of sufferings and unhappiness, not life styles or social conduct as such. For this reason each person can practise without in any way losing their traditional culture and individuality. Nichiren Shoshu also preserves a fundamental spirit or identity throughout the world and is embraced freely by individuals without oppressing any race or culture.

The reader is asked to make allowances for differences of style and approach between contributors. The book is a compilation of articles, lectures and essays given or written by a number of people at different times.

Nichiren Shoshu has developed many specialised words. In editing this text the aim has been to keep these to a bare minimum and to use colloquial English where possible. As an aid, footnotes have been used for unfamiliar words as they arise in the text. There is also a short glossary at the back. References have been numbered in the text and are given at the end of each article. Only a portion of the total writings of Nichiren Daishonin has been published in English, as *The Major Writings of Nichiren Daishonin*, volumes one and two. Many of the articles in this book refer to writings not yet in English translation, in published book form. In these cases reference has been made to *The Japanese Collection of Nichiren Daishonin's Writings* (*Gosho Zenshu*, in Japanese). However, to keep the references at the end of each article simple, reference to writings published in English is made simply as *Major Writings*. Reference to the Japanese original is to the *Japanese Collection*.

A brief historical sketch

About 3,000 years ago in India, Shakyamuni, the first historically recorded Buddha, left his secular life as a prince in order to find a solution to the four sufferings of birth, old age, sickness and death. He attained enlightenment and taught for over forty years to people he met, according to their circumstances and understanding. His teachings are therefore many and varied, and sometimes paradoxical. But in the last eight years of his life he taught his most profound teaching, the *Lotus Sutra*. When he taught the *Lotus Sutra* he asked his disciples to 'honestly discard all previous teachings'[1]. In Sanskrit, the *Lotus Sutra* is called *Saddharma Pundarika Sutram*.

After Shakyamuni's death, Mahayana Buddhism (see note on facing page) gradually spread through Tibet to China. It was translated into Chinese by a great translator called Kumarajiva. From there Buddhism spread to Korea and Japan. This all took place over a period of roughly 1,500 years.

During those periods when Buddhism flourished, peaceful and prosperous societies were established in India during the reign of Ashoka the Great, China during the T'ang Dynasty, and in Japan during the Heian period.

About 1,000 years after the death of Shakyamuni, established Buddhism started to decline. It had become formalised and ritualised so that only monks and those endowed with wealth and leisure could undertake the life-time of austerities which practice involved. It had lost its power to give happiness to ordinary people and the time was ripe for a great new teaching, or new approach, suitable for the present age which Buddhism calls the latter period of the Law. Shakyamuni had foretold this gradual decline in the power of his own teachings and predicted the persecutions which the votary of the true teachings for the latter period of the Law would experience. Nichiren Daishonin underwent exactly these persecutions, and this is one of many specific reasons for calling Nichiren Daishonin the true Buddha for the age in which we live (see 'latter period of the Law' in the glossary for further explanation).

'Everything has its essential point and the heart of the *Lotus Sutra* is its title, Nam-myoho-renge-kyo... A Law this easy to embrace and this easy to practise was taught for the sake of all mankind in this evil age of the latter day of the Law.'[2]

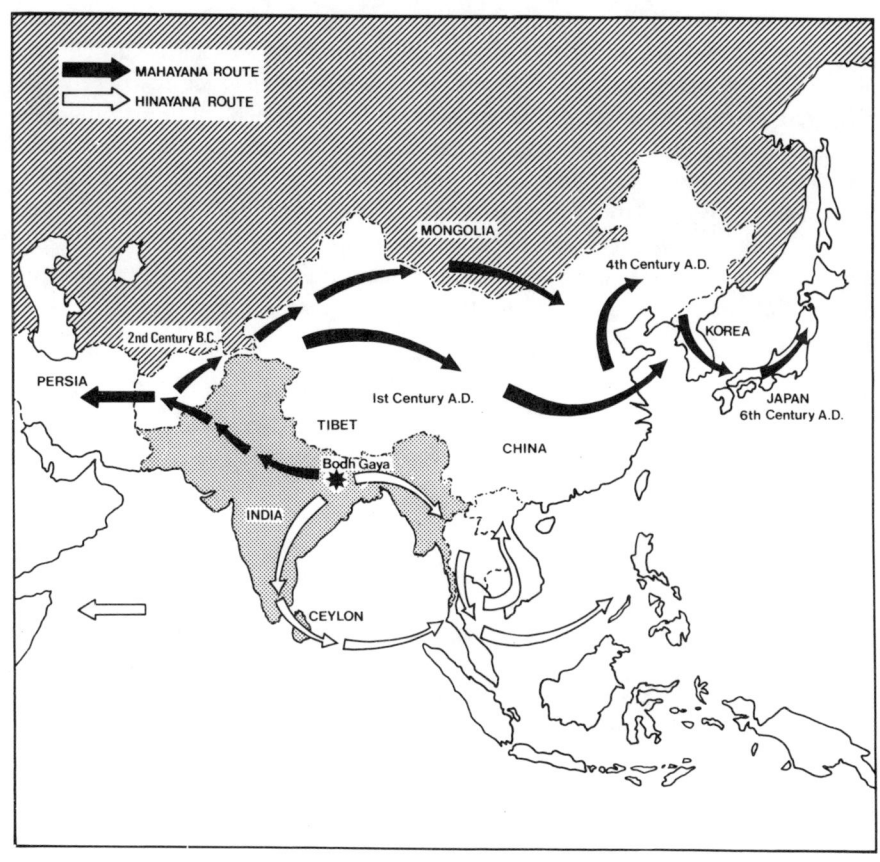

Spread of Buddhism during the two millennia following Shakyamuni

Note: Mahayana literally means the greater vehicle. Mahayana Buddhism is one of the two main streams of Buddhism. 'Vehicle' indicates a teaching or means to carry people to enlightenment. The Mahayana teachings are so called because they stress the importance of leading all people to enlightenment. Hinayana literally means the lesser vehicle. About a century after Shakyamuni's death, schisms began to form among those spreading his teachings. Those with a more conservative view held strictly to doctrine and ritual as originally formulated; this was the Theravada school (later termed Hinayana by Mahayana Buddhists).

Nam-myoho-renge-kyo was first expounded by Nichiren Daishonin (see footnote) on 28th April 1253 in Japan. He was the son of a fisherman and received his education through a temple, a common practice in those days. Nichiren Daishonin entered the priesthood and studied Buddhism widely before declaring that Nam-myoho-renge-kyo was the correct teaching for this time period. He was thirty-two years old. On 12th October 1279, twenty-seven years later, Nichiren Daishonin inscribed his enlightened life-condition on a great mandala called the Dai-Gohonzon. He dedicated the Dai-Gohonzon to the happiness of all mankind having spent a lifetime expounding his teachings which enable ordinary people, living ordinary lives, to attain the same enlightened state.

FOOTNOTE *Daishonin. Title given in Nichiren Shoshu to the Buddha for the latter period of the Law. Daishonin signifies the Buddha who establishes the essential teachings of Buddhism in the present age as distinct from one who seeks to spread the earlier teachings of Buddhism.*

REFERENCES
(1) *Lotus Sutra* Chapter 2
(2) 'The One Essential Phrase' *Major Writings* Vol. 1, page 222

Part 1.
The Buddhist View of Life

Song of youth

Though clouds dot the sky
and the wind blows
the sun rises again today
The eight a.m. sun of youth
holding within itself limitless power
as it spreads its light abroad, advances on correct course

Never deviating from its strict orbit,
beyond mansions of the sky, filling the heavens,
a king in glory
the sun advances wordless, unspeaking

Wisdom that is in fact ignorance, decline of culture
mechanisation of man, death of philosophy
scheming authority, deceit, trickery —
is it not to dispel these
that it sends forth its golden rays
that it advances in this lordly manner?

A sculpture of men and women in their entanglements
a globe whose contentions never cease
a world caught in the agony of indecision and revolt
human existence, the brilliance of its life all but extinguished
beneath the machinery of oppression —
the sun advances through the heavens
drawing forth a new vitality

Daisaku Ikeda

Nine consciousnesses

by Edward Clark and Chris Roman

The concept of changing destiny is perhaps one of the deepest principles at the heart of Buddhism. To understand this principle and the radical departure it takes from traditional Western thinking, perhaps it would be wisest to examine two ancient allegories which are very similar and yet profoundly different; one arises from Western culture and the other from the Buddhist tradition of ancient India. They are the stories of Oedipus and King Ajatashatru.

These two stories of patricide, one of the most heinous of crimes, have very different conclusions. The crux of the contrast is in the differing attitudes towards destiny expressed in each tale.

The story of Oedipus is a classic in Western literature. Dramatised almost 2,500 years ago by Sophocles, it tells the story of a tragic figure caught up in his own fate. Oedipus is the son of King Laius of Thebes and his wife, Jocasta. King Laius, fearful because he believes the prediction of a prophet that he will die at the hand of his son, abandons the infant Oedipus in a forest; the baby is rescued and raised by King Polybus of Corinth.

As a young man, Oedipus pays a visit to the Oracle at Delphi which tells him he is destined to kill his father and marry his mother. Distraught by this prophecy, Oedipus vows never to return to Corinth and his supposed family and begins to travel. In the course of his wanderings he has a quarrel with a stranger and kills him. Eventually, Oedipus ends up in Thebes where he rids the city of the Sphinx and wins the throne, together with the hand of the widowed Queen, Jocasta.

Years go by and a plague strikes the city. Having been told that it is caused by the fact that the murderer of the old King Laius is still at large, Oedipus sends for a blind seer named Teiresias to root out the murderer. At this point, one revelation after another unfolds as Oedipus discovers that the stranger he killed years ago was in fact Laius, his real father, and that he has indeed married his mother.

Overcome by these shocking discoveries, Jocasta kills herself, while Oedipus gouges out his own eyes and goes into exile. This tragic story of patricide, maternal incest and ultimate suffering is a classic example of the Greek tradition of man's subordination to his destiny and, in modern times, has come to underlie a basic Freudian theme of repressed love, hostility and guilt known as the Oedipus complex.

The story of King Ajatashatru, in contrast, starts before his birth as Mi Sho'on; the second heir of King Bimbisara. King Bimbisara desperately wants a son to succeed him. He visits a prophet and is told there is a hermit wizard in the mountains who, in his next incarnation, will be born again as Bimbisara's son. Impatient for an heir, King Bimbisara sees to it that the hermit dies by depriving him of food. At the moment of the hermit's death, Bimbisara's wife becomes pregnant. Then the prophet tells Bimbisara that his new son will bear a grudge against him because of the murder of the hermit. The prophet goes on to say that because of this grudge, Bimbisara's son will eventually harm him. Bimbisara names his son and heir Ajatashatru, meaning enemy not yet born. Terrified by the predictions of the prophet, Bimbisara tries unsuccessfully to kill the baby. Although unwanted, Ajatashatru grows up to become strong and healthy. One day Ajatashatru meets Devadatta (the arch-enemy of Shakyamuni), who tells the prince about his father's action to secure an heir and the predictions of the prophet. Devadatta does this because he wants to replace Shakyamuni as the leader of the Buddhist order and gain the support of Ajatashatru, the heir to the king. With this news, the negative impulses in Ajatashatru are stimulated. In a fit of indignation and rage, he has his father thrown into prison. Once in prison, Ajatashatru refuses to let his mother bring food to Bimbisara; an ironic repetition of the circumstances in which Bimbisara once starved the old hermit.

Finally, Bimbisara dies, and Ajatashatru eventually feels great regret. In his subconscious there is a conflict between his conscience and the reality of what he has done. This deep struggle in his psyche becomes more and more severe until it wracks Ajatashatru with emotional anguish and even affects his body with the contraction of leprosy. Ajatashatru goes to a doctor named Jivaka for a cure, but he can do nothing. It appears that it is his destiny to die. Jivaka suggests, however, that Ajatashatru goes to see the Buddha, Shakyamuni. At the same time, his father's voice seems to come to him saying, 'Go to see Shakyamuni, go to see Shakyamuni'.

At this point in the story of King Ajatashatru, the differerences between his tale and that of Oedipus begin to crystallise. Ajatashatru's actions are born out of grudges that exist at birth; an indication of the belief in rebirth and continuing karma. They differ considerably from the actions of Oedipus which seemingly have their basis in some kind of uncontrollable destiny; a fate to which no real cause is ascribed. In addition, the voice of his father urging him to go to see Shakyamuni, as well as the reactivated grudge stimulated by Devadatta, are both internal calls to action; subconscious motivations that ultimately become action. Oedipus, on the other hand, seems to act out scenes in a play already written by the mysterious and detached hand of fate.

When Ajatashatru hears the voice of his father, his underlying motivations become conscious. He is awakened to go and see Shakyamuni. The story continues with the Buddha taking Ajatashatru to meditate with him. Together with Shakyamuni in the moonlight, Ajatashatru finds that his mind, for the first time, becomes peaceful and clear while his leprosy is cured. The moonlight is a metaphor for the light of the Buddha's wisdom which illuminates the dark recesses of Ajatashatru's life.

Occasionally referring back to these two parables, we can delve into the process of changing karma a little more deeply.

Buddhism teaches that within every human being is the life of Buddha or enlightenment. The tendency however is for this enlightened state to be masked by negative impulses (see footnote) and to be thrown into the shadows of delusion and ignorance. The positive, dynamic energy of our Buddha state, when submerged by these negative impulses, tends to wane, leaving us with very little life-force and extremely susceptible to external influences; such as that exerted on Ajatashatru by Devadatta. Ultimately, this condition affects both conduct and appearance.

Buddhism teaches the eternity of life and the idea of rebirth. Buddhism also makes very clear the fact that our destiny, or fate, is a matter of our own creation; the effect of causes which we ourselves make (also known as karma). Taking the concepts of rebirth and karma together, we naturally come to the conclusion that even a new-born baby brings into this life effects of karma from previous existences. In this sense, the apparent innocence and purity of an infant may be only a superficial aspect of its life. At deeper levels there exist sources of pain, anguish, or even hostility that continue from a previous life (eg the grudge held by Ajatashatru).

Other philosophies might call this original sin and hold that it is a cause for lifelong guilt. Buddhism, on the other hand, states that karma is a natural outcome of the eternity of life and can always be changed. Equally, at any time during the life cycle, karma formed by past actions may surface just as it did when Ajatashatru met Devadatta.

In his 'Oral Teachings', Nichiren Daishonin said that King Ajatashatru was symbolic of people at the present time. Ajatashatru, for most of his life, was subject to the torments of his inner grudge. Similarly, all of us, at one time or another, are at the mercy of the fundamental darkness and blind impulses that are so deeply rooted in our lives due to our karma. Ajatashatru's murder of his father was an act motivated by his underlying anger, ignorance and greed. We too are susceptible to making such grave errors.

This may seem rather irrelevant because it is hard for many of us to think in terms of wanting to kill our fathers, however it really means that any

---

FOOTNOTE *Negative impulses, delusions or ignorance arising from desires. Termed collectively as* bon'no *in Japanese (see Introduction). For a fuller explanation see later article, 'Transforming the dark side of life'.*

human being is potentially capable of evil. This potential may lie dormant for most of our lives. Depending on our karma, however, it can be activated by a stimulus at any time. 'Unthinkable!' we might shout and yet how many of us at times have honestly felt almost uncontrollably violent impulses? How many of us have met people for whom we have a bad feeling for seemingly no reason? These experiences are evidence in themselves that there is much going on deep inside us of which we have little awareness.

The tale of Oedipus ends tragically, with no real attempt to explain his motivation. Ajatashatru meets a different end as he changes his fate after meeting with the Buddha. The story of King Ajatashatru illustrates the principle of transforming the dark side of life into Buddhahood. This does not mean that a person's enlightenment directly stems from darkness within his life. In dealing with these deep-seated negative desires, a Buddha seeks the noblest, and strongest positive forces that lie at the core of existence.

The key to understanding or controlling our destiny lies in comprehending the different levels of human consciousness. In the story of Oedipus, as mentioned before, no attempt was made to ascribe anything that happened to motivation forming out of consciousness. Things were simple: what happened, happened; what was perceived was acted upon; and what was predicted came true, as if by magic or the will of the gods. Ajatashatru, however, was driven by a number of things; totally obscure memory traces from a previous life, subconscious feelings of hostility towards his father and, ultimately, overriding sensations of guilt that drove him toward Shakyamuni together with other subconscious cues (ie the inner voice of his father).

Buddhism explains the different levels of human consciousness in terms of nine consciousnesses. The action and behaviour that makes up daily life and which are played out through the first five consciousnesses (to see, hear, feel, smell and taste), find their motivation in the sixth and seventh consciousnesses. The sixth is comprised of awareness, perception and judgment concerning external matters (e.g. this is edible, that is not). This, in turn, is influenced by input from the seventh, which is the realm of abstract thought involving judgment between good and evil and consciousness of the self or ego.

It is at the sixth and seventh levels that our lives experience the heavy influence of negative impulses, delusions or ignorance arising from desires. This influence first pollutes our seventh consciousness and then is carried to the sixth, with little or no awareness on our part that anything is amiss. In reality, however, by the time we start acting on our motivations, we have already been greatly swayed by these forces.

These negative forces originate in the eighth consciousness, similar to what Jung terms the collective unconscious. Jung defines the collective unconscious as the storehouse of latent memory traces inherited from man's ancestral past, a past that includes not only the racial history of man as a separate species, but his prehuman or animal ancestry as well. The collective unconscious is the psychic residue of man's evolutionary development, a residue that accumulates as a consequence of repeated experiences over many generations. It is almost entirely detached from anything personal in the life of the individual and is seemingly universal. All human beings have more or less the same collective unconscious. There is a distinction, though, between the collective unconscious and the eighth consciousness. Although the ideas are similar, it is important to realise that they are not identical. Jung's theory is used because it is the only school of psychology that matches the depths, but not necessarily the contents, of Buddhist philosophy. For Jung, the broad universality of the collective unconscious comes from the biological similarity in the structure of the brain in all races of men which, in turn, stems from a common evolution.

Buddhism, on the other hand, states that the infinite and universal aspects of the eighth consciousness stem from the eternity of life and the fact that the eighth consciousness serves as a storehouse for the eternal happenings of the first seven; the eighth consciousness is also capable of playing back effects through all of the seven consciousnesses at any time.

Every experience we have no matter how big or small, no matter how significant or meaningless, whether it be getting married or blowing our nose, is registered in the eighth consciousness and is available at some time to have an effect in our lives. This refers not only to the experiences of this life, within recent memory, but goes back to infancy and, even before, to previous lifetimes. Ajatashatru's eighth consciousness registered the murder of the hermit (his previous incarnation) by his father, although he, both consciously and subconsciously, had no realisation of it.

The eighth consciousness is where we have registered any one of the innumerable effects we have in our lives for which we seemingly have no explanation. Nichiren Daishonin stresses that the eighth consciousness is a storehouse for all three existences of life; past, present and future. Nothing is forgotten, erased or missed. Everything in our existence is inscribed at the eighth level of consciousness.

The eighth consciousness is like the repository of our karma. Many times people who practise Nichiren Shoshu refer to any turmoil in their lives as coming from their karma. It is easy to imagine that an 'earthquake' at the eighth level of consciousness (an upsurge of effects being released from storage) can really shake up the first seven consciousnesses, wreaking havoc with our perception, our motivations, and the way we interact with people and our environment.

In the case of King Ajatashatru, the fact that his motivation in imprisoning his father stemmed from darkness and desire at the eighth level is congruent with the effect in his body of the same negative forces; specifically his contraction of leprosy. Many doctors agree that some of the most difficult diseases to treat are those that accompany birth. The Buddhist explanation for such karma at birth is that it is caused by the immediate appearance of the negative life-condition stored in the eighth consciousness and carried over from a previous life. It is strange, and highly relevant, that some diseases are easy to treat while some remain untreatable. Moreover, two people with identical symptoms may react in totally different ways to the same treatment. This too is because of karma; the contents of the eighth consciousness.

Up until now we have been speaking of the purpose and contents of the eighth consciousness as though they are generally negative. This is not entirely true, and such examples have been used to illustrate the eighth consciousness and the origins of destiny. All human beings are born with the seeds of negative impulses, delusion or ignorance at the eighth level, and some people are heavily influenced by them. However, positive forces as a result of past action reside in the eighth consciousness as well. What creates a genius at birth or a child with an aptitude for music? These positive seeds eventually blossom beautifully at the conscious levels, but originate from the eighth consciousness.

Having taken a look at the Buddhist view of consciousness from the standpoint of the eight consciousnesses, we arrive at a point where we must go further. After all, because the eighth level is only capable of feeding back effects transmitted through the first seven consciousnesses, it would seem that the causes (ie thoughts, words, and actions) being made would continue to stem from a balance of positive and negative forces at the eighth level. This would lead to a cycle of both good and bad events in the life of the human being which, although varying in content, would seem very close to the sort of inescapable and unchangeable destiny that confronted Oedipus.

The concept of the ninth consciousness demonstrates the profundity of Buddhism. This teaching goes beyond any philosophy or any school of psychology. In uncovering the ninth consciousness, Buddhism gives us the key to changing our destiny. The ninth consciousness is the fundamental, pure sense; the original, purifying force that constitutes the essence of our lives.

It was this fountain of mercy and wisdom which Ajatashatru sensed welling up within himself when he met Shakyamuni. He glimpsed this power by coming temporarily into contact with the deepest level of consciousness. In meeting Shakyamuni, Ajatashatru was able to penetrate the cloud of ignorance and delusion on the eighth level. This might seem to be contradictory to what we said previously; that nothing is ever erased in the eighth consciousness. This is true, but negative impulses come from the fundamental darkness inherent in one's life. This darkness in Ajatashatru was totally illuminated by the light of the ninth consciousness; the light of Buddha-wisdom.

The essence of Buddha-wisdom is not an external illumination; it was not a pure shining beam that emanated from Shakyamuni onto Ajatashatru. It was the pure inner wisdom of Buddhahood that existed within Ajatashatru and exists within each of us. In doing battle with his inherent darkness, Ajatashatru discovered, with Shakyamuni's help, the life of Buddha within himself. This light dispelled the darkness in his psyche and allowed him to change his karma.

This is exactly what happens when we apply Nam-myoho-renge-kyo, the essence of Buddha-wisdom, to our own lives. This light of wisdom and compassion illuminates our bad karma and allows for a transformation of destiny. The practice of Nichiren Shoshu becomes the source for changing one's karma for the better. No matter how deeply karma may be rooted in the eighth level, it can be exposed and changed through Nam-myoho-renge-kyo.

By clarifying the eight consciousnesses, Buddhism explains destiny and the accumulation of karma through cause and effect, operating sometimes on conscious levels, but more often from subconscious motivation which we can barely, if ever, perceive. However, Buddhism also expounds the ninth consciousness and the process through which we can create fresh, new direction by utilising the dormant power of Buddhahood within our lives.

Nichiren Daishonin actually established a practical method for tapping the life of Buddha that underlies everything. In doing this, he provided the key to changing our destiny. His accomplishment is remarkable. Not only can we come to understand ourselves but we can also cope with our negative impulses. The difference between Buddhism and a theoretical philosophy is like the difference between knowing about mining and actually striking it rich. No longer need we worry about the problems of our ego as it plays out motivations and agonises over turmoil taking place at the sixth, seventh and eighth levels. We can realise the self of the Buddha, which is the ninth consciousness in all human beings.

Cause and Effect

by Daisaku Ikeda

The people and the society of our age might be compared to a ship in the middle of the ocean which has lost its compass. Without an accurate guide to lead them, they sail aimlessly along towards the future.

Everyone hopes to lead a happy life. For this reason, people throughout the ages have sought religion and various theories have been expounded as to how to become happy. In reality, however, how many have ever succeeded in realising their objective? There is a widespread tendency throughout society to belittle human life. I cannot help but believe that this trend originates from ignorance about the principle of cause and effect.

Economics has its principles. Science has its criteria. Likewise Buddhism has discerned the Law or fundamental principles at work in all phenomena in the universe. A passage in the collected writings of Nichiren Daishonin reads:

> 'There are shadows in the darkness, but man fails to discern them. There are routes in the sky by which birds fly, yet man cannot see them. Though invisible to us, there are certain currents in the sky and in the ocean for birds and fish to follow'.[1]

Likewise the principle of causality may remain imperceptible to the eyes of us ordinary people. Another passage states:

> 'A person writing at night may put out the lamp, but the words he has written still remain. It is the same with the destiny we create for ourselves in the threefold world.'[2]

Although we cannot see the words because of the darkness, they nevertheless remain written. Similarly, according to the principle of cause and effect, the karma we have formed remains an inseparable part of our lives.

We ordinary people tend to be engulfed by the rapid changes of society, caring only for praise or to avoid blame. However, as long as we allow ourselves to be carried away by such continual flux, we can never expect to obtain a sure guarantee of happiness. A passage reads:

> 'If you want to understand the causes that existed in the past, look at the results as they are manifested in the present. And if you want to understand what results will be manifested in the future, look at the causes that exist in the present.'[3]

Causality as taught in Buddhism is strict. It permeates the past, present and future. Furthermore, it is not something imposed on us by others, some god for example. Both causes and effects are entirely of our own making. All our actions without exception are imprinted in our lives as either good or bad karma.

The law of causality is invisible, but each single moment of our lives contains all phenomena in the universe including ourselves, cause as well as effect, without exception. Therefore it is described as strict. If things we are dealing with are tangible, we may be able to contrive various ways of evading them. The common law of society and the law of the land fall into this category. In contrast, the universal Law is a net which no one can escape. No matter what deception, disguise or cunning we may employ, we can never expect to slip through this invisible net.

'Letter from Sado' by Nichiren Daishonin states the following with regard to cause and effect:

'One who climbs a high mountain must eventually descend. One who slights another will in turn be despised. One who deprecates those of handsome appearance will be born ugly. One who robs another of food and clothing is sure to fall into the world of hunger... This is the general law of cause and effect.'[4]

No matter where we may be, we always live with the karmic retribution of everything we have done in the past. Because we are governed by the general law of causality, we will be forced to agonise under the harshness of our karma throughout our lives. There will be nothing but total darkness ahead, and we, as common mortals, will find it impossible to change our destiny. For instance, Buddhism condemns killing. One who takes life (the most precious treasure in the universe) whether it be another person's or his own, is certain to receive the retribution of being killed in this existence or the next.

However, this is a shallow view of the law of cause and effect and if this were all that Buddhism taught, we would have to consider our destiny fixed and unchangeable. We would be compelled to live passively and timidly, lest we commit some evil act or other. Nichiren Daishonin's Buddhism goes far beyond the general law of cause and effect by teaching a supreme Law which enables people to break through the fixed chain of causes and effects by opening up the Buddha nature innate within them, which is untouched by karma.

Most people are unknowingly, but profoundly, affected by their destiny or karma. Some are at the mercy of their fate. Others, battered by their own destiny, lapse into a life of resignation. As long as they remain ignorant of the causal law they will have no choice but to repeat the cycle of birth and death in this turbulent sea of suffering. In order to change this tragic destiny of mankind, Nichiren Daishonin established the Buddhism of the essential cause:

the cause to manifest one's innate Buddhahood. It enables the pure life-force of the Buddha state, which has existed within us from time without beginning, to well forth in an unceasing current. It changes all the tragic causes and effects that lie between and unveils the pure causes and effects which exist from the beginningless past towards the present and future. This is liberation from the heavy shackles of destiny we have carried from the past. This is the establishment of free individuals in the truest sense of the term.

REFERENCES

(1) 'Reply to Lady Nichinyo' *Japanese Collection* page 1250

(2) 'Rissho Ankoku Ron' *Major Writings* Vol. 2, page 44

(3) Shinjikan Sutra, quoted in 'The Opening of the Eyes (II)' *Major Writings* Vol. 2, pages 197-8

(4) 'Letter from Sado' *Major Writings* Vol. 1, page 40

Transforming the dark side of life

by Yasuji Kirimura

The darkness or negativity inherent in human life is referred to in Japanese as *bon'no*. It includes:
human desire which can turn into destructive greed;
a pessimistic, resentful outlook which has anger at its root;
instinctive behaviour which takes no account of reason;
an arrogant attitude to life;
lacking confidence, being fearful, doubting oneself and others;
holding to wrong ideas about the nature of life, ie acting without regard for the principle of cause and effect.
This list is literally endless, since human life can express itself negatively in so many ways. It could for example encompass irritability, a tendency to bear grudges and so on. These are all experienced in life, but emanate from a deeper level inside us.

A life of suffering is a life filled with negative impulses, delusion and ignorance. *Bon'no* inspires action which creates bad karma. The effect of this bad karma is then experienced as further suffering, which in turn aggravates *bon'no*. Inherent negativity, karma and suffering are called the three paths. One leads to another; there is a reciprocal relationship of causality among them. Inherent darkness in life gives rise to more bad karma, which produces more suffering and so on. It is because they are trapped in this cycle, that people have to endure suffering.

Suffering is caused by bad karma, and bad karma is produced by inherent negativity. Therefore to transform suffering into happiness and bad karma into good, one must first transform *bon'no*. People tend to think that their sufferings are caused by factors in the external world, but Buddhism maintains that the fundamental cause lies in negative impulses, delusion and ignorance inherent in one's own life. There can be no positive transformation of one's destiny without breaking the mutually destructive relationship between suffering, *bon'no* and karma.

An early form of Buddhism taught that we must confront and rid ourselves of all desires, and that only in this way can we attain enlightenment. The body was regarded as the source of desire and therefore austerities (such as fasting) were taught to control and subdue the body. Of course, desire can bring about suffering, but it is simplistic to dismiss desire as wholly evil. As long as we are alive, we are bound to have desires; they are necessary to sustain life. Some examples are the instinctive desire for food, sleep, and sex. Without desires, we die.

Another school of Buddhism originally held that all common mortals have the potential to become Buddhas. With the passage of time however, this doctrine degenerated to the point of asserting that common mortals, just as they are, are Buddhas, and their negativity, just as it is, is enlightenment. These Buddhists maintained that since negative impulses, delusion or ignorance are originally inherent in life, there is no point whatsoever in confronting or challenging them. Ritual prayers were established for acquiring wealth and satisfying sexual desire. This view of *bon'no* put sole emphasis on the point that negativity is inherent in life. It lost sight of Buddhism's original premise that the dark side of life causes great suffering.

Yet another Buddhist sect taught that negative impulses, delusion and ignorance are evil, but regarded them as unique to the human world, and not to be encountered in a 'Buddha land'. These Buddhists define this world as an 'impure land' because it is polluted by *bon'no*, and aspire to attain the Buddha's 'pure land' when they die. This view also avoids confrontation with negativity. Furthermore, teaching people to aspire to a transcendental realm outside daily life tends to weaken society by directing man's attention away from social problems and breeding apathy.

In contrast, Nichiren Daishonin's Buddhism teaches people how the dark side of life can be transformed into enlightenment; in other words *bon'no* and enlightenment are inseparable.

> 'Even without extinguishing *bon'no* or denying the five desires (desires arising from the five senses), they can purify all of their senses and eradicate all of their misdeeds.'[1]

In the phrase 'the dark side of life is transformed into enlightenment' the words 'transformed into' do not mean that negative impulses, delusion or ignorance are in themselves enlightenment. Negative impulses are negative impulses, and delude the mind.

Just as it is an error to think that the manifestations of negativity, just as they are, are enlightenment, it is also mistaken to think that all forms of inherent negativity are evil and should be eradicated. These two extremes are transcended by the principle taught in the *Lotus Sutra*, which is that without eradicating inherent negativity which has an essential purpose in life, it can be transformed into enlightenment. This principle has been illustrated with the metaphor of the lotus flower which blooms from a muddy swamp. Without mud, there is no lotus flower. The muddy water is necessary to sustain the life of the lotus, but the lotus is not the muddy water itself. The 'Oral Teachings' read, 'Now Nichiren and his followers who chant Nam-myoho-renge-kyo... burn the firewood of earthly desires (*bon'no*) and reveal the fire of enlightened wisdom'.[2] Because inherent darkness exists, enlightenment can be attained, as this passage very simply indicates.

Our lives are filled with the workings of negativity. However, even without eradicating it, we can purify our lives and attain enlightenment. *Bon'no* indicates illusion. Enlightenment indicates clear penetration, or an awakening to the truth. As we raise our fundamental life-condition, what functioned as a destructive tendency begins to function as enlightenment, and that which produced suffering begins to produce joy. What makes this possible is the power of Nam-myoho-renge-kyo. As we tap the Buddha nature through Buddhist practice, our negative tendencies are naturally directed towards happiness. This breaks the negative cycle of *bon'no*-karma-suffering and makes possible a transformation of our destiny.

REFERENCES
(1) *Lotus Sutra* Epilogue quoted in 'Earthly Desires and Enlightenment' *Major Writings* Vol. 2, page 229
(2) 'Oral Teachings' *Japanese Collection* page 710

How people affect their environment

by Barbara Cahill and Dick Causton

The basic cause for many of mankind's recent problems such as pollution, misuse of natural resources and present applications of nuclear technology is a lack of understanding of the deep and vital relationship between human beings and their environment.

Ecology is concerned with the interaction between living organisms and their physical environment. This relationship is clarified by the Buddhist concept of the inseparability of man and his environment.

Nichiren Daishonin explained in his writings that the environment and the living entity it contains are absolutely inseparable. He likened a human being to the body and the environment to the shadow. When the body bends, the shadow bends also. Likewise, the environment supports life. This means that while man is supported and influenced by his environment, he can also influence and change those same surroundings. Daisaku Ikeda takes the view that,

> 'The environment is the gravitational force of all the stars in heaven, the light energy of the sun, the web made up of ecological threads, the effects of nature and society upon people, etc. All these influences are co-ordinated and unified in the human personality.'[1]

Science is well aware that the environment has an immense effect on people. In medical science, for example, research has revealed how infectious diseases can be transmitted. There is even some acknowledgement of the influence weather has on people, impending snow causing a feeling of uneasiness in the stomach, and an east wind causing tension and dryness. Yet although these phenomena have presumably been experienced by human beings since they evolved on this planet, they were not officially recognised by medical science in its earlier days because they could not be proven scientifically. Now, scientists are beginning to know how life began through the action and reaction of simple elements. Also, through sociology and psychology we are beginning, for example, to understand the effects of tower blocks on the minds of the people and the problems of the child-parent relationship.

The absolute inter-dependence of any living being and its environment is becoming clearer, certainly so far as the environment's effect on us is concerned. But the extent to which we human beings can affect our environment, is still often not clear. We know the environment can easily affect us and we may even have believed it can give us lasting happiness. This, of course, is not so. The environment is always changing. What may be fortuitous for us today may have disappeared by tomorrow.

Greater emphasis must be placed on the way in which human beings can influence their environment. When the body bends, the shadow bends also. Human life is supported by the universe and because of this man can live physically and perform mental functions. However, it is no less true that if man lacks the active ability to react positively to and absorb all the beneficial effects from the environment, his ability to live may itself become threatened. For example, one may eat nutritious food, but if his digestive powers are weak, he cannot assimilate it. Thus, he is unable to build a strong body. Similarly, the most precious book is useless to one who cannot read it. The book will remain mere printed paper to him. Since human lives and their environments are inseparable, the self-activating force of human life creates and reforms its own environment. This principle emphasises the possible reformation of any environment by human life, therefore what matters most of all is that we ourselves should be solid and strong at the centre of our environment, basing our lives on the highest state.

How can we achieve this highest state of human life and thus make sure our environment reacts in the highest state as well? This is what the practice of Buddhism is all about. This is the key to happiness. If we reveal Buddhahood in our own lives, every facet of our environment will reflect Buddhahood in return. On the other hand if we live a life filled with greed, anger and stupidity, then these will be rampant in our environment too. This is self-evident in the way man, in his pursuit of profit, has polluted the land, sea and air and upset the world's ecology.

The foreword to the book *The Human Revolution* by Daisaku Ikeda reads:
> 'A great revolution of character in just a single man will help achieve a change in the destiny of a nation and, further, will cause a change in the destiny of all mankind.'[2]

Even on the level of scientific reality this is no longer as fanciful as it once may have seemed. Developments in the area of subatomic physics have resulted in the Buddhist theory of the 'oneness of the entity and its environment' becoming accepted by the world's physicists.

As Dr Fritjof Capra explains in his book *The Turning Point*:
> 'This is how modern physics reveals the basic oneness of the universe. It shows that we cannot decompose the world into independently existing smallest units. As we penetrate into matter, nature does not show us any isolated basic building blocks, but rather appears as a complicated web of relations

between the various parts of a unified whole. As Heisenberg expresses it, "The world thus appears as a complicated tissue of events, in which connections of different kinds alternate or overlap or combine and thereby determines the texture of the whole".[3]

Thus this principle postulated so long ago in Buddhism becomes reality on the scientific level in the 20th century. Its importance to those who practise Buddhism, however, is determined by how much each person can realise in his own life the extent to which he can dramatically and positively affect his environment for the better by his own deep inner change.

This universe of which we are a part is an incredible, vibrating world containing a myriad other entities, each one of which is a living organism in itself with its own particular environment. Yet all these environments overlap one another. As Daisaku Ikeda explains in his book *Dialogue on Life*:

'... the vibration of each individual human life affects all other types of life, and even alters the undercurrents of a people's consciousness... Human minds, when filled with love, trust and mercy, will naturally lead nature, an entity of life, to function vividly and creatively.'[4]

Buddhism teaches that you cannot separate any living being from its environment. This is an extremely important and profound concept, the understanding of which urges us towards a more constructive way of life.

REFERENCES

(1) Daisaku Ikeda *Dialogue on Life* Vol. 1, page 38

(2) Daisaku Ikeda *The Human Revolution* Weatherhill 1974

(3) Fritjof Capra *The Turning Point* Wildwood House 1982

(4) Daisaku Ikeda *Dialogue on Life* Vol. 1, page 54

The fusion of reality and wisdom

by Sue Thornton

In a television interview, Paul Tortellier, the famous 'cellist was asked by the interviewer, 'Has playing music taught you anything about life?' Without pausing for a moment's thought Tortellier replied, 'Through playing the 'cello and playing with other musicians I have learned that to enjoy life, you must know how to play your instrument really well'. He then added, 'It does not matter what instrument we play, what matters is that we all play in the same key'.

The capacity to create value in life depends on the fusion of objective reality and subjective wisdom. Tortellier's 'cello is the objective reality, he himself having the subjective wisdom, or ability to play it. The 'cello and the man produce a fusion of the two things. The result is fine music.

In the case of Tortellier, he is an outstanding musician playing a fine instrument, thereby creating beautiful music; separated they can create nothing. If Tortellier offered his 'cello to a five-year old boy, he would probably produce nothing resembling music. Alternatively, we could ask Tortellier to fly an aeoplane, and he would probably never get it off the ground. What is required is the inter-action between the ability to create value inherent within Tortellier as the subject, and the corresponding value capable of being produced by the object, the 'cello. When subject and object are perfectly fused, something of great value is created.

There are many ways of relating to our surroundings to produce something valuable. However, only limited human potential is tapped by any single relationship. The fusion between wisdom and reality derived from Buddhist practice, however, opens up a much wider area of creativity. It reaches the essential nature of each individual and taps the richest source contained within a person and this has a far-reaching influence over his inter-action with the outside world.

How is this possible? The extent to which wisdom is drawn out of an individual depends on what object is relating to what subject. Most objects have their limitations. They may produce, with human application, certain creativity; they may produce some self-knowledge or happiness in the process.

It was in order to show the full, limitless potential of human life that Nichiren Daishonin inscribed the Gohonzon (see footnote). This scroll, or mandala, can be described as the objective reality of Buddhahood or the external reality that encompasses all the power of the universe. The Gohonzon can exist only because every human being has the same rich condition within, even though it is latent and undeveloped.

Nichiren Daishonin inscribed, in an objective form, the Buddhahood that he realised from within his own life and which he knew to be inherent in all life. As the 'cello brings out Tortellier's musical creative ability, the Gohonzon, representing objectively the highest condition within man, brings out the universal wisdom often untapped within human life. This is called Buddha-wisdom. Chanting to the Gohonzon reveals this condition. The Gohonzon is the perfect mirror of this inner potential.

FOOTNOTE *The Gohonzon. See glossary and later articles. The Gohonzon is the physical manifestation of the Law of life. Nichiren Daishonin inscribed the Gohonzon to enable mankind to attain the same condition of enlightenment that he himself attained.*

Ten states everyone experiences

by Barbara Cahill

It is very difficult to understand what life really is. As we look at our own lives, we find moment by moment changes. We may wake up feeling full of the joys of spring. A letter we receive can enhance that feeling or put us into a rage. The journey to work can have the same effect. Once at work our mood will be influenced by what we have to do and what sort of temper everyone else is in. If we happen to have a bad day, a couple of drinks may bring us temporary relief. Travelling home may annoy us again, while our favourite meal or TV programme could make us calmer once more. These changing attitudes are explained by the theory of the ten states (or worlds) changing into one another.

Buddhism teaches that our experience of the world and our own inner life can always be expressed in ten basic states. They exist potentially within each of us and we experience them through inter-action with the environment. Each of these ten states has the potential to change into any of the others, so that no matter what state we may be in, we can bring forth another state in a moment.

Buddhism calls the lowest of the ten states hell. Hell is continuous torment and anguish. We cannot initiate action or affect our situation in any way; we are severely restricted. This brings incredible frustration and anger.

'The world of hell is essentially anger or indignation. Uncontrollable anger is an impulse innate in life, which tries to destroy not only one's own being but others as well. Therefore, the agonising state of hell is the greatest and deepest agony of all. Nichiren Daishonin penetrated the truth of hell and defined it as anger.'[1]

Time spent in hell seems interminable but the space of hell is minute. For instance if we have toothache we can think only of that and our sense of space, our thoughts and perceptions are as small as the tooth itself.

In the second state called hunger, desires dominate us. Even if a desire is satisfied we are only temporarily appeased before hungering after something else. Of course, like any of the ten states, hunger can have good and bad results. Hunger for knowledge has been the driving force of material civilisation and the inspiration behind technical progress. But as greed it has led to war and pollution.

Instinct is the basis of the third state, called animality. It signifies a day-to-day existence without thought for the results of action. Our outlook is one of stupidity because reason, wisdom and volition, are all dominated by instinct. We present no clear picture of ourselves to others. We are at the beck and call of those we consider superior, while we dominate those weaker than ourselves.

'Creatures thrive at the expense of other creatures, cutting to pieces the intertwined cycles of life among them, eventually destroying the foundation that supports their own lives. Today man has driven other living creatures to extinction by following the law of the jungle.'[2]

The fourth of the ten states is anger. We have the impression of being bigger and better than everyone. Everything and everyone else is small and trifling. We have an insatiable desire to win, and look for conflict and competition. We believe we are stronger than anyone else and this often has disastrous results. We like to appear benevolent and trustworthy, but in our hearts we have no respect for others and despise them. We look for a chance to challenge and destroy them.

'He who is in the world of anger, motivated by the warped desire to win at everything, despises others and tries to justify and value himself above all else. He is like a hawk, sweeping the sky in search of prey. He may have superficial benevolence, righteousness, propriety, wisdom and sincerity and seem to have some kind of moral sense, but his heart remains in anger.'[3]

The Sanskrit for the fifth state of tranquillity means creatures who can think. In Nichiren Daishonin's Buddhism it means the tranquil, humane state most natural to man. The state of tranquillity is characterised by behaviour which might be said to be fair and unaffected. A person in the state of tranquillity desires peace and happiness. We respond to the mores and codes of society, having more freedom and a surer foundation for action than in the previous four states. However, since we are emotional we cannot stay permanently in the state of tranquillity, even though this state is very natural to us. An adverse effect of this state is that, being peaceful and calm, we are lulled into not making effort to realise our full potential.

In the state of rapture, the sixth state, we feel buoyant, as if walking on air. This state comes about when what we desire is achieved. There are three levels of satisfaction: rapture one feels when fulfilling (i) material and physical desires (ii) social desires and (iii) spiritual desires. The third type of rapture is related to our spiritual flow. Here our psychic energy is high, we enrich and expand our lives (often through self-realisation and creativity). Time seems to fly past, and we are intensely aware. But if we lose what we have gained, rapture can easily collapse. Because of the good fortune and influence characteristic of this state, we may find ourselves in a very powerful position politically, in business, or community life. But inherent in rapture is negligence and carelessness. These undermine our character and mean that we are not able to fulfill what we have led society to expect of us.

Even though they each have positive characteristics, these six states are called lower because a person in whom they are the basic tendency is not realising his full potential, but is wandering weakly from state to state depending on the conditions around him.

The four remaining states are known collectively as the four noble worlds because we have to make effort to attain them and once attained we gain a deeper satisfaction. Although we must make this effort to experience these four states, once we have succeeded, we become more humane because we can at last shape the direction of our lives, instead of drifting helplessly from one to another of the six lower states.

The state of learning is characterised by reflection. Here we must have an open and sincere mind. If, when we go to work, we are concerned only with time-keeping and getting the work done, we cut ourselves off from the state of learning and remain in the lower six states. As soon as we try to apply ourselves to the work, using it as a source of future growth, we are in the state of learning. Learning is not just the prerogative of scholars and intellectuals. Anyone who has a seeking mind can bring out this state.

The state of realisation is inclined towards cultivating and polishing the self. It is a self-awakening to some truth or principle brought about by our relationship with someone or something. The emphasis here is on our creative nature, a spiritual awakening because we intuitively perceive something. Great philosophers and scientists have often written of their sudden intuitions. Such awakenings often lead to a total revolution in a person's thoughts and life. This is not exclusive to artists and philosophers. Anyone can refine himself and develop his intuitive wisdom if he makes enough effort and disciplines himself.

As soon as someone in learning or realisation achieves what they have set out to do and experiences the peak of joy, they are vulnerable to conceit and egoism. If our lives are strongly influenced by these two states we may find that our insight and attitude of self improvement leads to arrogance and stubbornness. We become self-satisfied and think we know it all. We may feel we have escaped from the six lower states and that we are better than the people in those worlds. As soon as we believe this we will be gripped again by the lower states of life.

People in learning and realisation often attain positions of prominence in society. If then they begin to be influenced by their negative qualities, they can become destructive, and this could, because of the respect accorded them, have an adverse influence even on the entire world. One example of the negative aspect of learning and realisation is the difficulty of maintaining a seeking mind with regard to Buddhism. As soon as we have grasped various principles we are likely to decide that we understand the nature of Buddhahood and we stay with the theory of enlightenment rather than pushing ourselves to actually attaining it. Many people have a natural tendency towards theoretical stagnation. To attain the highest state of life this must be challenged.

The ninth state, called bodhisattva, is where one makes effort for the happiness of others, at the expense of comfort, or even life itself. It is close to the positive qualities of maternal love. This state is based on the principle that true happiness is derived from action which takes away another's suffering and gives joy. We take on and feel another's suffering as if it were our own.

Yet even this noble state has its negative tendency. Helping others can very easily develop into self sacrifice in which a person places himself at a level above those who are in need, causing him to sink immediately into the lower states of life.

Many professions such as medicine and education offer great opportunity for bringing out the state of bodhisattva. But the essential nature of bodhisattva is found in the lives of those following the path of the bodhisattvas of the earth (see footnote) who, in the *Lotus Sutra*, vowed that they would risk their lives to spread Buddhism at the time we now live in, thereby enabling others to realise their own Buddhahood, and to establish their own eternal, indestructible happiness.

> '... The original mission and essence of the bodhisattvas of the earth is to maintain the fundamental Law called Nam-myoho-renge-kyo and stand on their own in actively contributing to the happiness of themselves and of other people and society... The value of a man does not depend on his fame, status, or authority. Is it not proper to say that the true value of a man depends on the great goal for which he lives an energetic life?'[4]

Daisaku Ikeda has described the double effort of those following the way of bodhisattvas of the earth towards their own inner development and to help others.

> 'Most important in accomplishing the ultimate purpose is to discover a method to cultivate oneself through benevolent, humane acts and thereby unlock the energy of compassion that will well up from the depths of one's life. One must reform himself through action and inner change. He must continue always to be humane and benevolent to others and at the same time to draw out his inherent life force to make his

FOOTNOTE. *Bodhisattvas of the earth. Reference to innumerable bodhisattvas who appeared in the 15th chapter of the* Lotus Sutra *and pledged to propagate the Mystic Law in the latter period of the Law.*

efforts fruitful. By a double effort both inside and outside one's life, he can build a solid foundation upon which he can live fully and with integrity, never yielding to difficulty.'[5]

A person in the state of Buddha, the tenth and highest state, may appear to be very ordinary, yet the awakening of their inherent Buddha nature leads them to the source of cosmic life force.

'They are able to understand all phenomena of life in the universe and the ultimate Law underlying them, including everything in the world and society. By drawing on the source of the cosmic life force, their own life force becomes unlimited, able to permeate the entire universe. Then they have true freedom. Such a life state is the full manifestation of Buddhahood.'[6]

The aspiration for Buddhahood exists in a realm even deeper than the desire for existence. Because it lies within the deepest sphere of each individual life, it is hard to perceive. The energy within the depths of life which seeks to integrate with the cosmic energy is the deepest impulse we have and, believing in its existence, we must begin to open it up until we experience it as Buddhahood.

REFERENCES

(1) Daisaku Ikeda *Dialogue on Life* Vol. 1, page 155

(2) Kitagawa in *Dialogue on Life* Vol. 1, page 164

(3) 'Causality within the Ten States of Life' *Japanese Collection* page 430

(4) 'Religion is Man's Fundamental Force, to Humanize Culture *Seikyo Times* January 1972, pages 18-30

(5) Daisaku Ikeda *Dialogue on Life* Vol. 1, page 209

(6) As above, page 216

Revealing Buddhahood

by Barbara Cahill

Earlier forms of Buddhism took the view that you remained for a lifetime in whichever basic state of life you were born into as a result of your karma. The Buddhism of Nichiren Daishonin explains that a person's state of life can change from any one of the ten basic states to another at any moment. Our constantly changing experiences of life are accounted for by the principle that each of the ten states of life contains all the others. Therefore, no matter which state we are in, the enlightened state of Buddha can be brought forth.

When we practise Buddhism we do not become free of the six lower states. Although they can be so negative and destructive, they are an essential part of life and we live in them constantly. We reveal the Buddha-state through the other nine states. The question we can ask ourselves is, which of the ten states is uppermost and influencing our experience of the other worlds? For example, the rapture of the Buddha is quite different from the rapture of a person whose main tendency is the state of anger.

Regardless of the changing nature of life, the Buddha nature is unchanging and unaffected by karma. By manifesting the Buddha state in our lives, we establish a free identity. This means that our reactions are spontaneously based on our highest qualities and so call forth positive reactions from the environment and society. We do not transcend the nine worlds, we influence all of them, thereby expressing the positive aspects in each one. For instance, the unstable, unreliable nature of animality can show itself as an instinctive sensitivity to others. The intense fury of anger can become a passion for justice and the deepest sufferings of hell can be transformed into a deep understanding and sympathy for the sufferings of others.

It is difficult to discuss Buddhahood because it can either appear too simple or so ideal as to be impossible. However, it is a state which we can experience right now. Buddhahood allows us to master the fundamental principles of life; to realise that the activity of each moment is fused with the life of the cosmos; to understand daily life completely. It means that we can understand all people impartially and can lead anyone towards happiness. Through power and wisdom, we can create harmony amongst any disparate elements. In Buddhahood, our life force can subdue all evil within ourselves; it can change the quality of our desires from selfish to unselfish. Such a person appears to be ordinary, but he has a strong sense of responsibility and integrity.

His attitude is friendly and open; his thinking is flexible and he is compassionate, wise, creative and courageous.

Nichiren Daishonin's Buddhism explains that these qualities exist in each person's life. It is very difficult to bring them out. Probably the main reason for the difficulty is that we cannot believe that we have such potential. The most common attitude which keeps us from realising this potential is the idea that we will do so at some time in the future or in some more ideal situation, through some mystic experience or an incredible moment of realisation.

> 'The true significance of Buddhahood lies in opening the palace within one's own mind to manifest Buddhahood, the supreme state of life. This ideal state is not to be found anywhere else. It exists within each person who lives on undaunted by the harsh realities of life. The Daishonin teaches that he who has perceived this fact is a Buddha and that one who, ignorant of it, seeks to attain that ideal somewhere or some day in the future is a common mortal.'[1]

Other people and all aspects of society are absolutely essential to our attaining Buddhahood, for we cannot bring out this state in a vacuum. Most of the qualities of Buddhahood deal directly or indirectly with others and their welfare. This is a very important aspect of Buddhahood: it manifests itself as compassionate action.

The desire for Buddhahood is the most fundamental desire in life. This is why it brings such happiness and why the neglect of it creates such unhappiness. Challenging ourselves through Buddhist practice, not to escape difficulties but to use them to bring out Buddhahood, is the way Buddhahood will manifest itself. From the moment that our attitude is one of challenge rather than escape, our Buddha nature has a channel through which it can appear. 'Let there be no mistake about Buddhahood: it is not the result of some process which has reached a certain stage'.[2]

In other words, Buddahood is not to be thought of as a long journey which one embarks upon and gradually puts the finishing touches to some twenty or thirty years later. Buddhahood is the fundamental power to create value. By developing a creative approach, we are opening up our Buddha state. Often this means we must challenge habitual reactions through intensifying our Buddhist practice. When we become able to respond with wisdom or compassion instead of headlong fury, spite and jealousy, this very action is the Buddha state itself. Living in the state of Buddhahood is the greatest of all types of joy.

> '... nature, the earth, grass and trees, as well as people's faces and actions, everything is charged with joy. Each breath one takes and each movement one makes reveals joy, gratitude

and the dignity of being alive. In such a condition, old age, illness and death are no longer suffering. They, too, become sources of joy.'[3]

REFERENCES

(1) Daisaku Ikeda 'Creative Society' *Seikyo Times* May 1973, page 7

(2) As above, page 8

(3) Daisaku Ikeda *Dialogue on Life* Vol. 1, page 216

Three thousand worlds in a moment of life

by Pat Allwright and Jim Cowan

In Buddhism, the theory of the ten states is part of a much bigger understanding of life, which can be summarised in the phrase, 'three thousand worlds in a moment of life'. This means that each moment of life contains three thousand different facets which are, at the same time, a harmonious entity.

Such a view does indeed test the limits of our mental abilities. Yet a theoretical appreciation is not the main point. Nichikan Shonin, the 26th high priest of Nichiren Shoshu, explained the vastness of the concept in *The Threefold Secret Teachings*.

'On the one hand, the entire universe is contained in each life at every moment, and on the other, each life-moment permeates the entire universe. The life-moment is like a particle of dust that possesses the elements of all the lands in the universe, or a drop of water whose essence differs in no way from the vast ocean itself.'[1]

Prior to this the principle had been systematised in China during the sixth century by the Buddhist teacher Chih-I, known as the great teacher T'ien-t'ai (see footnote), as a way of grasping this essential teaching of Shakyamuni's *Lotus Sutra*. This understanding of life, communicated by Buddhas of different eras is nevertheless about the same thing; an all-encompassing explanation of life in all its manifestations. At the time of T'ien-t'ai people used to meditate on this principle in order to elevate their condition of life, but Nichiren Daishonin rendered it unnecessary to do this. Instead he enabled people to actually use the principle amidst the practical realities of daily life; through chanting Nam-myoho-renge-kyo to the Gohonzon.

The theory of the three thousand worlds helps us to understand what is unique about life in all its many and varied aspects. It defines the dynamics of life in three main ways. The first is the principle that each of the ten states contains all the others. The second is a way of seeing how they change from one to another and is usually known as the theory of the ten factors. The third

FOOTNOTE. *T'ien-t'ai (538-597). Founder of the T'ien-t'ai sect which expounded the doctrine of 'three thousand worlds in a momentary existence of life'. Noted for his classification of Shakyamuni's teachings. His profound studies of the* Lotus Sutra *were compiled in three major works: the* Hokke Gengi, Hokke Mongu *and* Maka Shikan.

element accounts for the uniqueness in the way the various states of life express themselves and is known as the theory of the three realms. When these three theories are combined they make up three thousands facets of a moment of life.

Ten States

Hell (suffering)
Hunger (dominated by desire)
Animality (dominated by instinct)
Anger (dominated by competition)
Tranquillity (neutral state of man)
Rapture (the state of joy)
Learning (joy of knowledge)
Realisation (joy of creation)
Bodhisattva (desiring happiness for others)
Buddhahood (enlightened state)

} Ten states each containing all the ten states ie 10 × 10 = 100

Ten Factors

Form (appearance, physical aspect of life)
Nature (mind, wisdom, spirit)
Substance (integral entity, essence, life itself)
Power (motivating power of life, inner force)
Influence (exertion of influences by thought, action, speech)
Inherent cause (cause inherent in one's life)
External cause (catalyst in environment which reacts with inherent cause)
Latent effect (potential effect, change within one's life)
Manifest effect (visible outcome of the effect)
Synthesis of all factors (consistency, integrity, unity, harmony, harmony of life)

} The ten factors ie 100 × 10 = 1000

Three Realms

Self (all physical and spiritual elements – form, perception, ideas, volition, consciousness)

Society (world of living beings)

Land (world of environment)

The three realms ie 1000 × 3 = 3000 worlds

A study of the ten factors helps to clarify why it is so difficult to perceive the true nature of life. T'ien-t'ai explained that some of these are physical, some non-physical and some both. Since we find it easier to perceive the physical side of life, we can easily think that this is all there is to life.

T'ien-t'ai explained that form and manifest effect exist only in a material sense; nature, inherent cause and latent effect exist only in a non-physical sense; substance, power, influence and external cause are both physical and non-physical. Substance or entity is the deep underlying self which harmonises mind and body. It cannot exist without physical and non-physical aspects; it exists through them. Power is invisible, but becomes visible through action. Influence is visible but its effects are not all physical. External cause is seen but the relationship we form with it is unseen.

T'ien-t'ai's analysis clarifies that which is easy to see and that which is more difficult to perceive. For example, if someone makes us angry it is easy to see him or her as an external cause. We therefore tend to think he or she made us angry. It is not easy to see the inherent cause within our own lives which made us react in that particular way. This is why we find it so difficult to see that the answer to all our problems lies in a revolution of the self.

All life is equal in that it has the ten states and the ten factors. However the differences between people become apparent when we study the three realms. These define differences between individuals, social groups, and their various environments. Differences existing between people are differences in form, perception, conception, volition and consciousness. The senses of a person in hell lead to conceptions and volitions which are rather different from a person in any other state. The consciousness and perceptions of, for example, artists are different and express themselves in the works they create. Similarly each individual as a total person is unique, frequently living in groups which both mirror that uniqueness and share common features. Indeed the social sciences exist to give order and a sense of the common workings of different kinds of social groupings. What the social sciences are not so good at coming to grips with is the equal, if not greater, tendency towards uniqueness and variety which is the natural expression of life.

The third realm consists of the natural environment. It is fairly apparent that the life condition of a group of people affects the environment in which they live. If we visit someone's home, and find it dirty, untidy and dismal it is very unlikely that we will find the people living there bright and cheerful. A thriving business will have a lively, purposeful atmosphere. On a larger scale, mankind's greed and selfishness have produced the modern phenomenon of pollution. In all these examples the character of the environment has its roots in the lives of the people. We can never exist without some sort of environment, because the environment is the basis for our existence. But the environment always reflects our state of life.

It is very important to appreciate the practical value behind the apparently complex view of life contained in the theory of the three thousand worlds. It encompasses the totality of life and yet it explains in a simple way how human beings can expand their lives, become happy and influence all aspects of the environment for the better. What permeates the three thousand worlds is a momentary existence of life. The very existence of life potentially gives rise to the three thousand worlds. But it is by no means assured that in practice we will manifest all three thousand worlds; only a life based on the Buddha state will naturally do this. Karma, inherent negativity, and suffering reduce the potential of our life experience. A life confined to say the six lower states can only experience a limited number of the three thousand worlds. Whether or not we can reveal our true and full potential is a matter concerning our fundamental life state.

How can a human being fulfill himself amidst the harsh realities of daily life? Fundamentally this question should be, 'How can the life moment of an individual expand to embrace all three thousand worlds?' The answer does not lie in theory. If we merely understand the three thousand worlds theoretically we are like a mechanic who is a passenger in a car when the steering fails. We know what is happening, but are powerless to prevent it.

'The practice revealed by the three thousand worlds in each moment of life is to embrace the highest ideal and determination; the determination to create an eternal, enlightened land in this trouble-ridden world. But without the constant effort to profoundly and positively influence all types of people and change their respective environments it will be impossible (to achieve this).[2]

The practical application of the three thousand worlds, and hence the achievement of the most fulfilled life possible for a human being, lies in the ability to expand our lives so that moment by moment it has the expansive, powerful qualities of the Buddha state.

REFERENCES

(1) Nichikan Shonin *The Threefold Secret Teachings* Vol. 6, page 20

(2) Daisaku Ikeda *Dialogue on Life* Vol. 2, page 95

What happens when we die?

by Akemi Baynes

We live and then we die. Many think of death as something dark, like 'the end'. Buddhism asserts that whilst all physical manifestations of life must decline and disintegrate, life itself cannot be destroyed. Death is the unseen state of life. It is the time when a person's entity gathers energy to take on a new visible form. This continual rhythm of physical appearance, followed by death, is the very rhythm of life itself. Indeed the characters *Myo-ho* (of Nam-myoho-renge-kyo or Mystic Law) mean just this. How does Buddhism view death? One starting point in answering this question lies in recent evidence in medical research.

Professor Raymond Moody, an American philosopher and psychologist, has run a clinic for ten years. During this time more than 200 people who in clinical terms have died, have started to breathe again and returned to life. His book, *Life After Life* [1], includes many of these experiences. Some can be classed as hallucinations but many of the stories seem to be true. With the numerous examples there are many similar factors. Firstly, at death, life leaves the physical body and floats above it and, regardless of the condition of the body, there is still consciousness, sight and hearing. There, as if on a screen in front of you, you see what you did, what you felt, and what you thought throughout the whole of your life. All this happens very fast and as you see it, you are able to feel joy for the good things and deep suffering for the things you want to hide. Thirdly, in this place, you feel you meet other people who have died. However, there exists some line between this world and the unknown world and before you cross over, you can sometimes, according to these experiences, be pulled back.

Elizabeth Kubler-Ross originally did not believe in life after death. She made a special study based on experiences of the dying and her conclusions are similar to Raymond Moody's. She mentions particularly the part where the dead person sees everything that they did during their lifetime. She concludes that there is no such thing as a god to judge you; you judge yourself. She is convinced that death is only leaving matter and that life continues.[2]

There are of course theories about this thing that leaves the body at the time of death, which can see, hear and feel. Professor Okabe, a Japanese scientist, thinks that life after death is a form of energy, because energy is never destroyed:

> 'I think the main part of being is this particular energy and the physical body is a secondary factor. All physical matter changes in each person completely over seven years. If you think that it is the body that is the primary factor of life, then you are a completely different person to the one you were seven years ago. But this "energy" is constant, therefore everyone knows that they are the same person as when they were a child. This energy is able to function only because of the physical body. Death is only changing the form of energy. When you are alive, the energy is very active but when you die it becomes passive. It continues in a cycle between the two states forever'.[3]

Okabe's idea is very close to Buddhist thought. Buddhism says quite simply that this energy is life itself. Being alive or being dead are just different manifestations of life itself. This not only applies to human beings, but to everything throughout the universe.

The body, alive or dead, is also part of universal life. It is like rain that we see falling, which then disappears into the earth. The water drains underground, eventually flowing into a river and onwards to the sea. When this water evaporates from the surface of the sea it loses its physical form, until it again forms clouds and then rain. Because of our knowledge of science we know that the water itself does not change, only its physical form. In whatever form, it is still H_2O. From this example you could say that water as a liquid is like visible life and that the evaporated water is like death. The liquid and the evaporated water are just two cycles of the same substance. Similarly, life itself does not change, but it shows itself in two different forms, life and death, and just like the water, it will move in the cycle continually.

Despite the experiences of people who have died and then returned to life, it is impossible to know where life went to. This question is in the realm of philosophy and religion. It is something you cannot physically or scientifically prove. A famous Buddhist teaching by Vasubandhu (approximately 5th century AD) describes the experience of death and birth:

> 'At death, the body is separated into two, the seen body and the unseen body. This unseen body is called *sai-shin* which means "very small body" which cannot be seen by the physical eye. It is so small that it can move through any physical matter. The eyes, ears, nose and tongue keep perfect sense, not as a body, but as an ability. This small body is able to float and fly any distance instantly. Every life in this condition has the potential to be born again, but it cannot be born when and where it likes, it is decided by what the person did while he was alive. He is born in a situation or place

which is most suitable for the causes he made. At the moment when the female egg is fertilised by the male, if it is suitable for someone's new life, this "very small body" arrives there instantly, and a new physical form starts. When the physical body dies, it is impossible to change either the good or bad effects contained within its life. There is also no fixed time when it will be born again. For some it will be a very long time. It is all decided by what that person did during his life.'[4]

This teaching very clearly describes karma.

Buddhism goes deeper than psychology in asserting nine consciousnesses (see earlier article). The ability to hear, see, feel, smell and taste are the first five. The sixth consciousness is our conscious mind. The seventh is active both when we are awake and sleeping. This is the realm of abstract thought and judgment. All the latent feelings of the six consciousnesses appear in our dreams through this seventh consciousness. Near to death, the six consciousnesses become latent and the seventh appears very strongly. Within this seventh consciousness is the deep desire to live. At death, the eighth consciousness becomes the strongest, with the seven consciousnesses becoming latent. At the time of death all the seven consciousnesses, though latent, still exist or are stored within the eighth. The eighth level is where karma is stored during life. When life separates from the physical body, these seven consciousnesses continue to exist dormantly. The desire to live life again is still contained within the seventh consciousness. This will be the force to return to life again, but this will only be achieved in accord with the karma created by the causes made during the previous life through these seven consciousnesses, now stored in the eighth. When physical life starts once more, the seven consciousnesses again become strong, and the eighth level becomes latent.

Karma is every function of our lives, our thoughts, words and deeds (ie the workings of the seven consciousnesses) which are then carved into our lives. Our thoughts, words and deeds, whether good or bad, are not judged in the end by morals or the laws of society. Those based on the protection and development of life will be stored as good karma and those causing destruction, hurt or harm to life, as bad karma. This karma created within the seven consciousnesses is stored at the eighth level. Therefore, when you die, your life will be latent in the universe exactly as it was at the point of death and, since the seven consciousnesses are latent, they are unable to react to any environmental influence to change your life state.

We might imagine that life after death will be peaceful and a time of resting, but just as you can have a happy or unhappy dream, after death you can also feel joy or suffering. It is important, therefore, to look at one's present life very strictly. The Buddhist theory of the nine consciousnesses is concerned with how we can be sure to build up good and valuable causes with our seven consciousnesses so that there are plenty in store at the eighth level at the point of death. In this respect the importance of the ninth consciousness becomes clear. The ninth consciousness is described as the essence of universal and eternal life (Nam-myoho-renge-kyo), which can, if we choose to make the effort, permeate all the other eight consciousnesses.

The process of dying brings to the fore the main tendency of our lives. As one approaches the moment of death, one's life centres on one of the ten states; the one which relates most strongly to his karma. After physical death we will remain in this state, latent in the universe, exactly as we were at the point of death.

If our lives are inclined towards suffering in the six lower worlds then we can expect to experience these in the latent state. The aim of Buddhism is to enable us to change the fixed direction which we have built up over many lifetimes. Buddhism is concerned with allowing us to bring forth the ninth consciousness, which is unaffected by this karma. Having done this in life, the ninth consciousness will remain predominant while dead. What happens when we die depends on what we do now to reveal the Buddha state.

REFERENCES

(1) Raymond Moody *Life After Life* Corgi 1975

(2) See Elizabeth Kubler-Ross *On Death and Dying* Macmillan 1969

(3) Prof Okabe *Daibyakurenge* June 1973, page 62

(4) Vasubandhu *Kusha-Ron*

Pursuit of the great middle way

by Daisaku Ikeda

In May 1972 and again in 1973, Daisaku Ikeda spent ten days in discussion with the prominent historian and scholar, the late Arnold Toynbee. Towards the end of these discussions, Daisaku Ikeda asked Dr Toynbee how he felt mankind ought to make the transition from this century to the next. Dr Toynbee's answer introduces this article and refers to the path of the golden mean as the most desirable path towards the 21st century. The article itself elaborates on what Buddhism means by the golden mean, or as it is also known: the great middle way.

'Man in the 20th century has become intoxicated by the power of technology. However, this same technology has poisoned our environment and led the human race towards self destruction. Man must gain the wisdom to examine and control himself. Therefore, we must be very cautious about the extremes of total liberty on the one hand and the suppression of the will on the other. We must walk the path of the golden mean. I feel this is the road which mankind must take in the 21st century.'

Arnold Toynbee

Mahayana Buddhism is based on the fundamental principle which Dr Toynbee described as the golden mean. Much of Western thought seems to have been directed towards either spiritualism or materialism. There is a third or middle way, which encompasses and sublimates both extremes. If it is this middle way which can put civilisation onto the proper path, what concrete measures are involved?

During the dialogue with Dr Toynbee it became clear to both of us that the most important step is to address ourselves to the basic root of all issues, namely what is man and what is the meaning of life? These questions necessarily led us to discuss the nature of life, in order to fully understand and clarify the most basic element which forms civilisation.

Sharing our experiences, we found ourselves in firm agreement that the most urgent task is for each person to instill in his heart a genuine and lasting respect for the dignity of life. The 21st century must be the century for life; an age when respect for life comes before everything else. Then and only then will we be able to transform our technological world into a new culture that is human in the richest, fullest meaning of the word.

At an early stage in the teachings of Buddhism, life was described as an accumulation of many kinds of suffering. These were represented by the four sufferings: birth, growing old, illness, and death. Obviously there are many other forms of suffering, such as the anguish of being destined to part from loved ones, or the frustration of seeking something in vain. Thus, Buddhism expounds that life is full of suffering.

When happy, we feel time passes quickly, yet happiness inevitably fades away. As this feeling of happiness is lost, it adds to our sorrow and so our suffering seems to last even longer. The differences between rich and poor, differences of race and ways of life, rather than giving man happiness, force man even more deeply to sense his own agony.

Why then do people feel such suffering in life? Buddhism explains that this is because people are unaware of the impermanence of all things in this world. That is, amongst all the phenomena in the universe or all expressions of life, none are eternal or unchanging. The young will grow old and anything physical will eventually deteriorate. All living things must die. Heraclitus stated, 'All things are in constant flux'. All the phenomena in the universe are like a flowing river which changes continually without a moment's pause. When we forget the principle of impermanence and come to think that the things in our lives will last forever, then this causes us to suffer.

It is only human to hope that the beauty and youth we have today will last forever. By the same token, I do not think that there is anyone who is working with all his might right now because he believes that he can take his wealth with him when he dies.

Such thinking is a perfectly natural expression of human emotion. Nevertheless it is because we have these emotions that we suffer. Since we want to keep those whom we love with us forever, we will certainly face the greatest pain of all when we finally part from them. Because people feel they must accumulate wealth, they attach themselves to it and even compete with others over it, and yet one day they must come to taste the bitterness of losing that wealth.

The problem of death is a similar one. It is an undeniable fact that we are alive now. We could not possibly go around thinking about death all the time. Unconciously, we act as if our lives will last forever, and we do everything possible to protect ourselves. On the other hand, it is this strong attachment to life that leads to all sorts of human suffering. It is because we fear death that we are afraid of becoming old or sick.

Buddhism teaches us that we should seek to clearly recognise these cycles of impermanence. It asserts that we must find the courage to accept them as fact. Instead of turning our eyes away or chasing after continually changing phenomena, we should perceive reality with detached objectivity, for therein lies the way to open the path towards true enlightenment.

Life is impermanence and hence, suffering. Moreover because we are flesh and blood we are certain to die. Buddhism teaches us to recognise the fact of death without fear and to discover that which is in the depths of life. It is not sensible to suggest that being entranced with the impermanent phenomena of life, or becoming a slave to one's desires, is in any way stupid. As long as we are attached to living, and, value life, we will want to do these things; they are natural human emotions.

Buddhism has been regarded as a religion which requires the individual to sever all connection with the passions and desires of this world. It has even been considered a hindrance to social and economic progress and to be in opposition to the advancement of civilisation. It is undeniable that today the countries which are conventionally regarded as Buddhist, lag far behind in the development of science and technology. Japan is an exception because she has concentrated on incorporating the framework of the Western technological revolution. The principle of impermanence is only one of many in the teachings of Buddhism. It is only one aspect of Buddhism, yet it has often been regarded as its entirety. Such an evaluation must be criticised for its one-sidedness.

The essential teachings of Buddhism by no means require the suppression of human desires or any denial of attachment to life. It is not a passive or nihilistic religion. Nor does it teach one to realise the impermanence of life, so that he may surrender himself to destiny. The actual core of Buddhism reveals the ultimate reality of life which produces all desires and attachment. It also expounds the eternal and unchanging Law, which gives unity and rhythm amidst impermanent and changing phenomena.

Each of us has a lesser self and a greater self. To be blinded by transient phenomena and tortured by desire is to exist only for the lesser self. To live for the greater self means to be enlightened to the Law of life, which expresses itself in all things, and maintain this enlightenment amidst the transience of the phenomena of the world.

Pursuing the greater self by no means implies giving up the lesser self. Rather the greater self gives new direction to the lesser self. Without the pursuit of wealth there would have been no economic growth. Without the will to overcome the natural elements, the sciences would not have developed. Without love, literature would have lost an enduring theme. One branch of Buddhism taught that all desires should be extinguished. For this purpose it even condoned self-immolation. Such an approach is not representative of the highest teachings of Buddhism.

Desire and sorrow are basic to life; they cannot be eliminated. Desire constitutes a generative, motive force in life. That is why the desires of the lesser self must be correctly orientated. True Buddhist teaching strives to discover the greater self, and instead of suppressing or eliminating the lesser self and its desires, it seeks to control and direct it positively. Where many people do this a direct contribution will be made to the creation of a better world civilisation.

From this it is obvious that Buddhism first clarified the principle of impermanence and taught people to face their own death, in order to let them understand the vivid reality of the eternal and unchanging law of the universe. A Buddha is not someone who encourages resignation, but a person enlightened to this eternal Law. The fact that he can face his own death without fear and clearly realise the transience of human life is because he knows that man's life is a precious existence, which has in its depths the eternal and unchanging Law.

A person controlled by desire and running in circles after the constantly changing world of phenomena, even if he fully uses his intelligence, is not essentially different from an animal living by instinct. Only when man focuses his attention on the invisible reality within the depths of the phenomenal world can he express the value in his life which is truly worthy of a human being.

Dr Toynbee regards desire which is controlled by the lesser self as 'diabolic desire' and desire which is fused with the greater self as 'loving desire'. He sounded a warning to the 21st century by stating that in order to control 'diabolic desire' it is absolutely necessary for each individual person to recognise and control his own inner self.

Our lives, as well as all phenomena in the universe, are like a great revolving wheel. However, the way we experience the turning of this wheel will vary greatly, depending on whether we are gasping for breath as we grapple with the quagmire of our desires, or whether we are rolling along smoothly on life's firm ground of enlightenment to the greater self. Only when the latter is the case will our civilisation be able to make sure and sound progress. Whether or not the 21st century will become the long dreamed of civilisation, which realises mankind's aspirations for happiness and well-being, depends solely on whether man can focus on human nature and discover the eternal, immovable, and constant reality within life.

We are now at the crossroads. The period before the end of the 20th century and the beginning of the 21st century is the time of transition. It is the time when man must decide whether or not to become human in a rich, full sense. It may be an exaggeration, but man does not seem to have progressed much beyond the status of an intelligent animal.

Within the 700-year-old writings of Nichiren Daishonin the phrase 'talented animal' appears. It is my belief that mankind must become more than an intelligent or talented animal. It is time for man to become active in a spiritual sense in relation to knowledge of the greater self and of universal life. This is the achievement which everyone should accomplish for themselves, today.

Part 2.
The Power of Practice

Theme

There is a theme to each opus
and in the theme joy and sorrow echo by turns
When one has captured the clear-cut shape of the theme,
an unparalleled masterpiece may be born

There are themes to human life
and when one has discovered his own particular theme
and as an actor given it the fullest expression,
a mighty dream will be born

This thing called life —
with sweat and thoughtfulness
as a novelist writes a novel,
with sweat and perseverance,
as a painter plies his brush,
seated before the blank paper of the instant and the future,
one creates a new portrait of oneself —
it is a vigorous task to be engaged in

Daisaku Ikeda

'On Attaining Buddhahood'

Written by Nichiren Daishonin in 1255 to one of his followers

If you wish to free yourself from the sufferings of birth and death you have endured through eternity and attain supreme enlightenment in this lifetime, you must awaken to the mystic truth which has always been within your life. This truth is Myoho-renge-kyo. Chanting Myoho-renge-kyo will therefore enable you to grasp the mystic truth within you. Myoho-renge-kyo is the king of sutras, flawless in both letter and principle. Its words are the reality of life, and the reality of life is the Mystic Law (*myoho*). It is called the Mystic Law because it explains the mutually inclusive relationship of life and all phenomena. That is why this sutra is the wisdom of all Buddhas.

Life at each moment encompasses both body and spirit and both self and environment of all sentient beings in every condition of life (see footnote), as well as insentient beings, plants, sky and earth, on down to the most minute particles of dust. Life at each moment permeates the universe and is revealed in all phenomena. One awakened to this truth himself embodies this relationship. However, even though you chant and believe in Myoho-renge-kyo, if you think the Law is outside yourself, you are embracing not the Mystic Law but some inferior teaching. 'Inferior teachings' means those other than this sutra, which are all provisional and transient. No provisional teaching leads directly to enlightenment, and without the direct path to enlightenment you cannot attain Buddhahood, even if you practise lifetime after lifetime for countless aeons.

Attaining Buddhahood in this lifetime is then impossible. Therefore, when you chant the Mystic Law and recite the *Lotus Sutra*, you must summon up deep conviction that Myoho-renge-kyo is your life itself.

You must never seek any of Shakyamuni's teachings or the Buddhas and bodhisattvas of the universe outside yourself. Your mastery of the Buddhist teachings will not relieve you of mortal sufferings in the least unless you perceive the nature of your own life. If you seek enlightenment outside yourself, any discipline or good deed will be meaningless. For example, a poor man cannot earn a penny just by counting his neighbour's wealth, even if he

FOOTNOTE *'Every condition of life'* ie any of the ten states or three thousand worlds.

does so night and day. That is why Miao-lo (see footnote) states, 'Unless one perceives the nature of his life, he cannot eradicate his evil karma' [1]. He means here that unless one perceives the nature of his life, his practice will become an endless, painful austerity. Miao-lo therefore condemns such students of Buddhism as non-Buddhist. He refers to the passage in the *Maka Shikan*, 'Although they study Buddhism, their views revert to those of non-Buddhists' [2].

Whether you chant the Buddha's name (ie chant Nam-myoho-renge-kyo), recite the sutra or merely offer flowers and incense, all your virtuous acts will implant benefits and good fortune in your life. With this conviction, you should put your faith into practice. For example, the *Jomyo Sutra*, (also known as the *Vimalakirti Sutra*), says the Buddha's enlightenment is to be found in human life, thus showing that common mortals can attain Buddhahood and that the sufferings of birth and death can be transformed into nirvana. It further states that if the minds of the people are impure, their land is also impure, but if their minds are pure, so is their land. There are not two lands, pure and impure in themselves. The difference lies solely in the good or evil of our minds.

It is the same with a Buddha and a common mortal. While deluded, one is called a common mortal, but once enlightened, he is called a Buddha. Even a tarnished mirror will shine like a jewel if it is polished. A mind which presently is clouded by illusions originating from the innate darkness of life is like a tarnished mirror, but once it is polished it will become clear, reflecting the enlightenment of immutable truth. Arouse deep faith and polish your mirror night and day. How should you polish it? Only by chanting Nam-myoho-renge-kyo.

What then does *myo* signify? It is simply the mysterious nature of our lives from moment to moment, which the mind cannot comprehend nor words express. When you look into your own mind at any moment, you perceive neither colour nor form to verify that it exists. Yet you cannot say it does not exist, for many differing thoughts continually occur to you. Life is indeed an elusive reality that transcends both the words and concepts of existence and non-existence. It is neither existence nor non-existence, yet exhibits the qualities of both. It is the mystic entity of the middle way that is the reality of all things. *Myo* is the name given to the mystic nature of life, and *ho* to its manifestations.

Renge, the lotus flower, symbolises the wonder of this Law. Once you realise that your own life is the Mystic Law, you will realise that so are the lives of all others. That realisation is the mystic *kyo*, or sutra. It is the king of sutras,

FOOTNOTE *Miao-lo (711-782). Ninth patriarch of the T'ien-t'ai sect in China. Miao-lo restored the sect, writing profound commentaries on T'ien-t'ai's major works, and contributing to the theoretical clarification of his teachings.*

the direct path to enlightenment, for it explains that the entity of our minds, from which spring both good and evil, is in fact the entity of the Mystic Law. If you have deep faith in this truth and chant Myoho-renge-kyo, you are certain to attain Buddhahood in this lifetime. That is why the sutra states, 'After my death, you must embrace this sutra. Those who do so shall travel the straight road to Buddhahood' [3]. Never doubt in the slightest, but keep your faith and attain enlightenment in this lifetime. Nam-myoho-renge-kyo, Nam-myoho-renge-kyo.

Respectfully
Nichiren

REFERENCES

(1) Miao-lo *Maka Shikan Bugyoden Guketsu* Vol. 4

(2) T'ien-t'ai *Maka Shikan*

(3) *Lotus Sutra* Chapter 21

The meaning of Nam-myoho-renge-kyo

by Pat Allwright

The title of the *Lotus Sutra* is Myoho-renge-kyo. Nichiren Daishonin added the word *Nam*, meaning devotion or dedication. Translated superficially, Nam-myoho-renge-kyo means, 'I devote myself to the inexpressibly profound and wonderful truth, the Law of life, expounded in the *Lotus Sutra*, which embodies the loftiest teachings of Buddhism'.

Nichiren Daishonin said:

'To practise only the seven characters of Nam-myoho-renge-kyo may appear limited, yet since this Law is the master of all Buddhas of the past, present and future, the teacher of all bodhisattvas in the universe, and the guide that enables all human beings to attain Buddhahood, its practice is incomparably profound.'[1]

In another writing he says:

'Since all laws and phenomena are included in the five characters Myoho-renge-kyo, the word *kyo* (literally sutra) is the crown of all the sutras. It thus envelopes all the sutras.'[2]

In other words, the title, Myoho-renge-kyo contains the essence of the teachings of the *Lotus Sutra* which itself contains all Buddhist teachings. 'The One Essential Phrase' explains the importance of the name. An extract reads,

'... included within the title, Nam-myoho-renge-kyo, is the entire sutra consisting of all eight volumes, twenty-eight chapters and 69,384 characters without exception.'[3]

Each Chinese character has a wealth of meaning which makes it the most suitable language for a written teaching. It is not possible here to study all the aspects of the meaning of Nam-myoho-renge-kyo because, as explained above, this would be to explain the entirety of Buddhist philosophy. What follows is only a basic outline.

Myoho is often translated as Mystic Law. Mystic implies difficult to discern. *Myo* refers to inherent enlightenment and *ho* to inherent ignorance. *Myo* refers to death and *ho* to life. *Ho* relates to all phenomena which can be seen or experienced through the senses, whereas *myo* relates to those aspects of life which are unseen. For example, if someone is very sad it is obvious from their facial expression and reactions. But when the same person becomes happy and starts laughing, where does the sadness go? We cannot say that it exists as it did before, but on the other hand it does still exist somewhere within that person's life and can reappear at some other time. This is called the state of 'neither existence nor non-existence', and is described as mystic. Thus life in all its myriad manifestations, both physical and non-physical, is following a continuous cycle of *myo* and *ho*, latent and manifest, death (the unseen or latent state) and life (encompassing birth, growth, and physical decline).

Myo has three more meanings which Nichiren Daishonin explained in 'On the Daimoku of the Lotus Sutra': to open, to be endowed and perfect, and to revive. The inherent energy of life is expansion. This is what to open means. To be endowed and perfect means that every element in life has this quality; for example, every drop of water in the ocean contains the properties and elements of the ocean itself. To revive refers to the regenerating and recreating force of life.

Myoho describes life in its entirety, which is difficult to comprehend and is therefore called mystic. *Ho* refers to individual phenomena whereas *myo* refers to the universal rhythm of life, which harmonises and unifies. *Ho* is the nine states, whereas *myo* is the Buddha state. Both aspects are, of course, inseparable. This is why a life based merely on *ho*, that is, on symptoms or outward appearances, tends towards defeat and destruction whereas a life based on *myoho* is always tending towards creativity and harmony.

Renge means lotus flower and signifies the simultaneous nature of cause and effect, since in the lotus the flower and seed pod appear at the same time. *Renge* indicates the simultaneity of *myo* (Buddha) and *ho* (nine states). In terms of our Buddhist practice the nine states are the cause and the Buddha state the effect.

There are actually two causes, the inherent cause and the external cause, and two effects, the latent effect and the manifest effect. We all have the inherent cause for enlightenment or Buddhahood. The external cause is the Gohonzon and our relationship with it is chanting Nam-myoho-renge-kyo. This instantly creates the manifest effect of Buddhahood and we also create a tendency (latent effect) to experience the Buddha state in the future. We should be clear that *renge* does not mean that we can live now and pay later. *Renge* explains the simultaneity of cause and effect which means we suffer right now when we act in a destructive way.

> 'As to the question of where exactly hell and the Buddha exist, one sutra reads that hell exists underground and another sutra says that the Buddha is in the west. However, closer examination reveals that both exist in our five-foot body. The reason I see it this way is that hell is in the heart of a man who inwardly despises his father and disregards his mother, just like the lotus seed, which contains both flower and fruit at the same time.'[4]

Finally, since the lotus flower blooms in muddy swamps, *renge* also signifies life's ability to purify itself.

Kyo has two meanings. The first is sutra, teaching, sound or vibration. Sounds never stop. Everything affects everything else in the boundless universe.

'*Kyo* denotes the voices and sounds of all living beings. One interpretation says, "voice makes an essential part of Buddhist practice". This is called *kyo* and the three existences of life are also called *kyo*.'[5]

Thus *kyo* also means thread as in the weft of cloth. This signifies continuity or the flow of past, present and future; the perfect teaching which explains the eternal flow of life.

Through this explanation, limited though it must be, it can be seen that *Myoho-renge-kyo* has infinite depth. All Buddhist principles and philosophy arise through deeper study of these characters. But how can we use it in our lives? *Myoho-renge-kyo* is a beautiful, all-embracing truth, but if it remains pure theory it is useless. This is where *nam* comes in.

Nam is derived from the Sanskrit word *namas* which means devotion or salutation. In Chinese it was translated as *kimyo*. *Ki* means to return to the unchangeable, unshakable truth, and *myo* (a different *myo* from that of *myoho*) means to be based on wisdom which functions according to circumstances. So the action of *nam*, devoting or concentrating ourselves on chanting Nam-myoho-renge-kyo to the Gohonzon, means to return to this unchangeable truth of Myoho-renge-kyo and then live our lives based on the wisdom which arises, according to whatever situations occur in our daily lives. In terms of action *kimyo* means to unify one's individual life with the rhythm of the life of the universe. Ultimately, happiness does not depend on anything outside us. A good job, marriage, or any other situation in life can just as easily be a source of suffering as it can be of happiness. This is why we chant Nam-myoho-renge-kyo: to ensure an unshakeable condition of life.

REFERENCES

(1) 'Earthly Desires are Enlightenment' *Major Writings* Vol. 2, page 228

(2) 'On the Daimoku of the Lotus Sutra' *Japanese Collection* page 942

(3) 'The One Essential Phrase' *Major Writings* Vol. 1, page 222

(4) 'New Year's Gosho' *Major Writings* Vol. 1, page 271

(5) 'Oral Teachings' *Japanese Collection* page 708

The power of Nam-myoho-renge-kyo

by *Takehisa Tsuji*

The previous article explains Nam-myoho-renge-kyo from a mainly theoretical standpoint. Nichiren Daishonin established Nam-myoho-renge-kyo as a practical way for all human beings to reveal the Buddha state. It is therefore important to know how to apply Nam-myoho-renge-kyo to situations which confront us in daily life. Because it explains Nam-myoho-renge-kyo from a practical standpoint the following article is rather different in style.

What is Myoho-renge-kyo? Nichiren Daishonin teaches that Nam-myoho-renge-kyo is found within the entire universe – even in the sun, moon and stars, the ocean and mountains, in trees, plants and rocks, in dogs and cats, and most certainly in human beings.

For example the light bulb was developed by Thomas Edison who understood the principle of electricity. We can say that the function of the light bulb is to light up your face, the carpet and every corner of the room. Along the same lines, there is the theory of electromagnetic waves. We cannot see these waves but there is a way to perceive them. If we turn on the radio or TV set, we can hear the words or see the picture carried by these waves. In the same way there exists a Law of life which we cannot see either, yet, as in the above examples, the principle takes shape and can be seen in none other than the Gohonzon. Just as the light bulb shines throughout the entire room, the benefit of the Gohonzon shines throughout the universe.

Rather than discussing the Law of the universe, I would like to discuss the same Law inherent in the human being. If we can understand ourselves, then we can understand the universe, for they are the same. This is because our lives are the life of the universe itself. Nichiren Daishonin says that what is important is to be able to see the workings of Nam-myoho-renge-kyo inside ourselves. As in the case of the light bulb or TV set, all we have to do is turn the switch on and the light or image appears. As we chant Nam-myoho-renge-kyo, the power of the universe wells up from within our lives just as if we were switching it on through our practice to the Gohonzon.

When we see a beautiful flower we feel the beauty of the flower. The flower that is outside brings about the feeling which comes up from within. Records and pianos are outside ourselves, but we enjoy their music from within ourselves. In the same way the Gohonzon that is outside ourselves brings joy from within. When we establish a relationship with the Gohonzon by chanting Nam-myoho-renge-kyo, that Nam-myoho-renge-kyo within ourselves will well up.

If we were to look at the Gohonzon while chanting, imagining that it is 'out there', thinking that by doing this 'I'm going to get something', it would be like begging for something. Even under these circumstances, we would probably benefit. However, it would be as tiny as the tip a waiter gets compared to the full payment for the meal. Nichiren Daishonin teaches us not to look for Nam-myoho-renge-kyo outside ourselves; rather we should let Nam-myoho-renge-kyo well up from within ourselves. Joy comes welling up from within. Darkness also does the same. When we are angry or hysterical, these feelings appear from within ourselves. When we feel sorry or sad about someone, these feelings also come from within ourselves.

Nam-myoho-renge-kyo is hard to perceive. It is like our eyebrows, which being so close to our eyes, are impossible to see. In fact, the Buddhahood of Nam-myoho-renge-kyo is within us. Therefore, it is important that we try to activate one hundred per cent of the Nam-myoho-renge-kyo from within ourselves. If we can chant with the greatest of joy, then Nam-myoho-renge-kyo will burst from within our lives naturally. If, however, we chant with the attitude that it is a waste of time, very little Nam-myoho-renge-kyo will appear in our lives.

Living is our own responsibility. Although we are responsible for our lives, it is a perplexing fact that we can never really see ourselves. To see one's face, one looks in a mirror. But with that same mirror we cannot see our inner selves. By placing the Gohonzon in front of ourselves and chanting Nam-myoho-renge-kyo to it, we are able to polish our inner selves. Just as we use make-up and adjust our physical appearance with a mirror, by chanting to the Gohonzon we can polish our inner lives.

We also come to realise that we can overcome illness by tapping the life-condition of Buddhahood within us. In other words Nam-myoho-renge-kyo does the work of medicine. Prescribed medicine usually functions to correct a specific malaise or physical problem. If we have difficulty with our eyes, we use eyedrops and if we have stomach ache there is something specific we can take. Whether we have a headache, cancer, an asthmatic condition or any other illness, as well as medical treatment, we should apply Nam-myoho-renge-kyo which has the deepest and most enduring healing effect.

When we chant Nam-myoho-renge-kyo we can overcome all our present difficulties. Nichiren Daishonin wrote, '... those who believe in the *Lotus Sutra* will gather fortune from ten thousand miles afar'. Therefore, we will find good fortune in the future as well. Nam-myoho-renge-kyo can be likened to a magnet which attracts happiness. The more confidence and joy we have, the stronger the magnet will become.

The Gohonzon: Life in the Buddha state
by James Perry

Those of us who practise Nichiren Shoshu Buddhism have a Gohonzon enshrined in our homes. The Gohonzon we cherish and practise to is a paper scroll on which are written many Chinese characters and two Sanskrit characters. Down the centre is written the essence of the Gohonzon: the oneness of the Law Nam-myoho-renge-kyo, and the Buddha, Nichiren. Surrounding this inscribed Law, are characters representing the basic states of life, various 'life-functions' and protective forces of the universe with which man should be in harmony. Negative functions of life are also represented on the Gohonzon. However, all these powers, illuminated by the seven characters of Nam-myoho-renge-kyo display the enlightened nature they inherently possess.

All aspects of life are displayed on the Gohonzon: good and evil, suffering and joy, ignorance and enlightenment. If the Gohonzon were only to show the Buddha state, Nam-myoho-renge-kyo, then this would not be an accurate reflection of life, because life is composed of desires and strong forces which are necessary for growth in a physical world. The Buddha state can be likened to the flower of the lotus plant, which lies white and pure on the water's surface. Desires are like the roots of the lotus which draw nutrients from the muddy floor of the pond. As the beautiful bloom of the lotus depends on its earthbound roots for its existence, so we can transform our negative impulses and desires in order that our lives can function and sparkle. Thus all life is represented on the Gohonzon bathed in the light of the Buddha state. Nichiren Daishonin declared that this is the true object of worship.

The ten states of life are all present on the Gohonzon (see earlier article). We experience one predominant state at any one time, whilst the other worlds remain inactive or dormant until such time as they are aroused. The state which was predominant then sinks into latency to be replaced by a new condition. For example, when we are offended by someone, the world of anger is awakened and becomes active, manifesting itself in the mind, the eyes, the mouth, the skin and indeed the entire body. We become bathed in the world of anger. Eventually the world of anger will subside and return to latency in the depths of our lives and another of the ten states will awaken.

It is further apparent that, whichever of the ten states we are experiencing, an external stimulus is always necessary. Taking the state of anger again as an example, we can see that it is only aroused from dormancy deep in our lives, when we experience something from our environment, that is, somebody saying something offensive, or our witnessing injustice in some form or other. This applies to all of the ten states. They can only be activated by our environment through such a relationship. No matter how hard we try to be angry, it is impossible to be so, unless an anger-producing condition exists outside us to activate it.

In our society there are numerous conditions occurring which regularly activate the six lower states. Furthermore we often realise that one state is activated more frequently than others. Hence some people are referred to as always angry or power-mad (animality) or constantly miserable (hell). In other words, a predominant life-condition is developed which centres on one of the six lower states and consequently brings us great unhappiness. We know that if we suffer from depression (hell), incessantly strive for wealth or power (hunger), or are critical of others (anger), we will be unable to consistently derive joy from life. Even if our predominant life condition consists of the states of learning, realisation and bodhisattva, our happiness is still relative and liable to change. For example, people in the state of learning can often become conceited with their own knowledge, whilst those in the state of realisation quite often regard themselves as exclusive and seek their own satisfaction irrespective of others. People in the state of bodhisattva frequently sacrifice their own happiness, and lacking the power necessary to achieve victory, become disillusioned and sad.

The purpose of Buddhism is very clear. It is to establish Buddha as the predominant state and cause it to manifest in human life. Nichiren Daishonin explained that, in order for hell or anger to be aroused, it is necessary for there to be a hell or anger-producing object. Therefore, for the state of Buddha to be developed, it is necessary for a Buddha-producing object to be present.

Because Nichiren Daishonin was enlightened, he was able to activate this highest state within the lives of his close followers. However, this situation could not greatly benefit the majority of people who were unable to meet and establish a personal relationship with Nichiren Daishonin. Therefore Nichiren Daishonin, in his mercy for all the people in Japan and the world who would come after him, inscribed his Buddha state on to parchment with these words, 'I, Nichiren, have inscribed my life in ink, so believe in the Gohonzon with your whole heart.'[1] Thus for the first time in history, a means was revealed by which all human beings, regardless of status, position, sex, race or ability, could attain happiness in this world, through their own efforts in their own environment. This was revolutionary. Previously the practice to attain enlightenment in the East was only open to those with the means to pursue a religious life, ie the nobility, or those devotees who had exceptional ability to endure the harshness and deprivation of monastic life.

The Gohonzon inscribed specifically for all mankind is called the Dai-Gohonzon and is today enshrined in the Sho Hondo (meaning palace or castle of the true Law) at Taiseki-ji in Japan. Since the passing of Nichiren Daishonin in 1282, sixty-seven successive high priests have received and passed on the heritage of the Law in a direct and unbroken line from Nichiren Daishonin, making it possible for people to have the means to develop the supreme condition of Buddhahood in their lives by chanting to the Gohonzon in their own homes.

Go of Gohonzon means honourable, *hon* means foundation and *zon* means to esteem: that is to say 'fundamental object of devotion'. In our practice to the Gohonzon there are three ways for us to gain full benefit. The three ways are mental, verbal and physical. Both good and evil can be manifested through these three aspects of human behaviour. Any or all of these three, when they are evil, engrave bad karma or misfortune in our lives. However, any of these three, when they are beneficial and especially when working together, engrave good karma or fortune in our lives. It is essential, therefore, for us to embrace the Gohonzon, not merely with mental reverence, but also with verbal invocation and physical action. When we mentally revere the Gohonzon, chant Nam-myoho-renge-kyo to it, physically sitting upright, with palms together, we activate the state of Buddhahood and manifest it in our lives. The other nine worlds, when Buddhahood is activated, blossom like trees and plants in spring when the sun appears, transforming their negative aspects into something positive and valuable.

In practical terms, the emergence of our Buddha nature gives us the power to overcome difficulties or stalemates in daily life and help others to do the same. To manifest the state of Buddhahood means to establish freedom by using our circumstances to grow and develop, rather than being limited or controlled by them. The result is a life filled with joy, wisdom and compassion which spreads outwards like ripples on a lake, in an ever-increasing contribution to our families and friends, and to society as a whole.

REFERENCES
(1) 'Reply to Kyo'o' *Major Writings* Vol. 1, page 120

The Gohonzon: An in-depth explanation

by Dick Causton

The previous article outlines what the Gohonzon is and what it means to us in daily life. The following article is also about the Gohonzon. It has been included for readers who wish to know in more detail what the many characters inscribed on the Gohonzon signify.

The word mandala means all-embracing or wholly protective. The term was first used in ancient India, thousands of years ago. It referred to a circle that was drawn in the sand around the place where a religious ceremony was going to take place. The circle not only surrounded the centre point of the ceremony, the object of worship, but also the people taking part in it. Its purpose was to mark off the area and protect it from any devilish influences. Later, the word mandala was used to mean a sanctuary; that is to say, the building where the object of worship was located, including those who wished to worship it. The word mandala was also used for a religious training centre.

When inscribing the Gohonzon, Nichiren Daishonin applied to it the exact meaning of the word mandala. The Gohonzon is conceived and inscribed in such a way that we too, when we devote ourselves to practising to it, are within it, embraced and protected by it.

Nichiren Daishonin explains in depth what is inscribed on the Gohonzon in this passage:

'The five characters of the *Lotus Sutra's* title are inscribed in the centre of the treasure tower (ie Gohonzon), while the four heavenly kings are seated at the four corners. Shakyamuni and Taho Buddhas, as well as the four leaders of the bodhisattvas of the earth, are lined across the top. Seated below them are the bodhisattvas Fugen and Monju, and men of learning, including Shariputra and Maudgalyayana. Beside them are posted the gods of the sun and the moon, the devil (see footnote) of the sixth heaven, the dragon king and Ashura; Fudo and Aizen take up their stations to the south and north, respectively. The devilishly treacherous Devadatta and the

FOOTNOTE *Devils, deities and gods. See later footnotes which explain the meaning of these terms in Buddhism. In general they refer to functions and forces inherent in human life and the universe.*

dragon king's ignorant daughter attend too. The demon Kishimojin appears with her ten daughters, who sap the lives of people throughout the universe. Also present are the guardian deities (see footnote) of Japan; Tensho Daijin and bodhisattva Hachiman, representing the seven ranks of heavenly gods (see footnote opposite), the five ranks of earthly gods and all other major and minor gods in general. As all the gods appear in their essence so must they appear in their manifestations.

The hoto (11th) chapter (of the *Lotus Sutra*) states, "All the assembly were lifted and present in the air". Dwelling in the Gohonzon are all the Buddhas, bodhisattvas and great saints, as well as the eight groups of sentient beings of the two realms who appear in the first chapter of the *Lotus Sutra*. Illuminated by the five characters of the Mystic Law, they display the enlightened nature they inherently possess. This is the true object of worship."[1]

'The five characters' refers to the title of the *Lotus Sutra* which, in Chinese characters, is *Myo ho ren ge kyo*. These are boldly inscribed down the centre of the Gohonzon, preceded by the two characters *na mu* meaning 'devotion to' and making a total of seven characters. Thus everything else on the Gohonzon is illuminated by the Law of life, Nam-myoho-renge-kyo. As in all Buddhist teachings, the title contains everything within that text or sutra.

Nichiren Daishonin then refers to the four heavenly kings. He placed these in the four corners of the Gohonzon (north, south, east and west) as guardians to protect the Gohonzon and all who chant to and respect it. These four heavenly kings mark the boundary of that ancient circle in the sand; the boundary of the great mandala. These kings represent, in ancient legendary terms, the protective force of the universe which guards those who strive to live in harmony with the Law. This protective force guards the Law itself, the people who are devoting themselves to practising and teaching it, and the place in which the Law is spread or taught. In other words all are embraced by the great mandala and wherever the Gohonzon exists, this protection exists too.

Nichiren Daishonin goes on to say that across the top of the Gohonzon are Shakyamuni Buddha, Taho Buddha and the four leaders of the bodhisattvas of the earth. As you look at the Gohonzon, Shakyamuni is on the left, and Taho is on the right. Shakyamuni represents the subjective wisdom that arises within us when we practise; Taho represents the eternal and unchanging truth, that is to say the objective reality of the universe. When we combine this reality with our subjective wisdom, in other words when our wisdom enables us to realise the eternal and unchanging truth of the universe, we can attain Buddhahood. We can achieve this fusion through sincere practice to the Gohonzon.

On either side of Shakyamuni and Taho, Nichiren Daishonin placed the four leaders of the bodhisattvas of the earth. They are Jogyo (who was the leader), Muhengyo, Jyogyo and Anryugyo. These four leaders represent the great qualities which develop and grow in our lives quite naturally through our practice to the Gohonzon. Jogyo represents the true self; not the shallow egotistical self, but the greater self in the depths of our lives. Muhengyo represents eternity; the eternity of our existence in the Buddha state. Jyogyo is purity; the way in which our perception is changed through purifying the five senses. Anryugyo is happiness; the indestructible happiness of knowing one's true or greater self. These great qualities quite naturally appear in our lives as we continue to practise.

In many countries of the world, etiquette demands that the most important person is placed on the right. If you understand Chinese characters it may seem strange, therefore, that when you look at the Gohonzon, the character for such an important figure as Shakyamuni Buddha is on the left. Yet, looking at the characters for the four leaders of the bodhisattvas of the earth Jogyo, the leader is placed correctly on the right. Etiquette is important to the Japanese and Nichiren Daishonin certainly did not make any mistakes when inscribing the Gohonzon. So what does this mean?

In the *Lotus Sutra* Shakyamuni describes dramatically how he first saw a vast treasure tower appearing, it was emerging from under the ground, reaching high into the sky. In this amazing and graphic allegory the great treasure tower, encrusted with precious gems, represented life with all its mystic and wonderful qualities. As it halted, floating in the air, the doors of the treasure tower opened and Taho Buddha could be seen sitting inside. When it became stationary in front of Shakyamuni, Taho invited him to step inside. Shakyamuni entered and then turned round, as it were facing us, sitting down in the place of honour on Taho's right, and together with him, looking out of the door towards us. Thus when we look at the Gohonzon it is as if we were looking at the two Buddhas through the door of the great treasure tower which has come to us through the air, with Shakyamuni facing us and Taho on his left.

On the other hand, the four leaders of the bodhisattvas of the earth are placed, as it were, with their backs to us, indicated by Jogyo being on the right, facing Shakyamuni and Taho, just as we face the Gohonzon. So also are all the other characters for the nine worlds which actually represent us human beings. It is as if we are looking, together with our leaders, the four great bodhisattvas, at the treasure tower which is Nam-myoho-renge-kyo. Thus, when we look at the great mandala, it is as if we are actually within it facing the great treasure tower of Nam-myoho-renge-kyo; just as in the *Lotus Sutra*, the bodhisattvas of the earth appeared and were addressed by Shakyamuni from the treasure tower, concerning their mission to propagate the Law in the age we now live in. When we chant to our Gohonzon, when we practise morning and evening, we are taking part in the eternal ceremony in the air, protected within the boundary of the great mandala.

> *'Seated below them are the bodhisattvas Fugen and Monju, the men of learning, including Shariputra and Maudgalyayana. Beside them are posted the gods of the sun and moon. . .'*

Nichiren Daishonin refers next to two of Shakyamuni's disciples. They are Fugen and Monju who represent all of Shakyamuni's other disciples. Fugen stands for those people who have the mission deep in their lives to protect those following the path of the bodhisattvas of the earth. These are people who live mainly in the state of learning, who can understand the various philosophies and teachings which exist, and who declare the greatness of Nichiren Daishonin's Buddhism even though they themselves do not practise. The other disciple, Monju, represents the power of wisdom in action within daily life.

Included next on the Gohonzon are those whom Nichiren Daishonin describes as the men of learning. These are represented by Shariputra and Maudgalyayana. The inclusion of these two disciples is significant, not only because all of the ten states are on the Gohonzon including these worlds of learning and realisation, but also because Shakyamuni had originally taught in his provisional teachings that men of learning and realisation were too conceited to be able to attain Buddhahood. However, in the *Lotus Sutra* and for the first time, he taught that even these disciples would attain Buddhahood.

Nichiren Daishonin goes on to talk about the gods of the sun and moon, which appear on the Gohonzon in the form of the gods (see later footnote, page 67) Nitten and Gatten, representing these powerful forces of the universe. The influence of all these universal forces can be either positive or negative, nourishing or destructive. It is very obvious that the sun can destroy us if we fail to use our wisdom. Whereas, of course, the sun is the greatest nourisher of this planet, providing the energy for everything to grow. We, too, need the sun to make us healthy. However, although these forces of the universe have a positive and negative aspect, on the Gohonzon they are all illuminated by Nam-myoho-renge-kyo. Therefore, through our practice to the Gohonzon, the positive side of these forces will be working in our favour.

> *'... the devil of the sixth heaven, the dragon king and Ashura; Fudo and Aizen take up their stations to the south and north, respectively...'*

Nichiren Daishonin mentions here the devil (see footnote) of the sixth heaven, the dragon king and Ashura. However, before dealing with these, it is best to

FOOTNOTE *Devil. In Buddhism, this word does not refer to an outside power or spirit. It means the destructive or negative force inherent in the life of man and all phenomena. That this devil exists on the Gohonzon, illuminated by the Mystic Law, means that we can transform our own evil or destructive tendencies into valuable ones.*

consider Fudo and Aizen. If we look at the Gohonzon, in the centre of the right and left hand side there are two Sanskrit characters. They look very different from the Chinese characters. These Sanskrit characters represent Fudo on the right as you look at the Gohonzon, and Aizen on the left.

Fudo represents the all-important Buddhist principle of transforming the sufferings of life and death into enlightenment. This is a natural process. As we practise, we discover, through experiencing the power of the Gohonzon, that we can use the four sufferings of birth, sickness, old age and death, for our growth. We can develop our true strength as human beings through these sufferings.

Aizen represents the great principle that negative impulses, delusion or ignorance arising from desires (*bon'no*) are transformed into enlightenment. Again this is a natural process. As we chant to achieve what we desire, the power of Nam-myoho-renge-kyo is so great that without us even realising it we are drawing out our Buddha state and transforming our lives.

Nichiren Daishonin used these Sanskrit characters mainly because the Gohonzon, although it gives proof of its power in daily life, must also be proof of the validity of Nichiren Daishonin's teaching in the flow of orthodox Buddhism from the time of Shakyamuni. Shakyamuni's Mahayana teachings were first recorded in Sanskrit, which was understood by scholars in all the countries of the known world at the time of Nichiren Daishonin. Therefore these two Sanskrit characters are symbolic of the eternal flow of Buddhism from the ancient past to the distant future and of its validity for all the peoples of the world.

'*The devilishly treacherous Devadatta and the dragon king's ignorant daughter attend too. The demon Kishimojin appears with her ten daughters, who sap the lives of people throughout the universe.*'

Now we can move on to the lower states of life, including the devil of the sixth heaven, the dragon king and Ashura, who were referred to earlier. Hell is represented by Devadatta, that cunning, vindictive and unhappy cousin of Shakyamuni, who yet, like all human beings, had the potential to attain Buddhahood.

Hunger is represented by Kishimojin, the female demon who had five hundred or more children and who, when food was short, thought nothing of killing other people's babies so that her children could feed on them. This represents the power of people's selfish desires. Through being challenged by the Buddha, she then realised the error of her ways. From then onwards she hungered only to protect all the children of the Buddha, signifying that we can also turn greed-centred hunger into hunger for justice and other great causes.

Animality is represented by the dragon king. Animality can be vicious, yet it is also an essential quality of life. On the negative side, animality is the bullying, aggressive state of instinctive self-preservation where the strong dominate the weak. Finally the state of anger is represented by Ashura. Although Nichiren Daishonin does not make reference to it in the above quotation, the state of tranquility is represented on the Gohonzon by Tenrin Jo-o, which literally means, wheel-rolling king. This represents the basic or neutral human state from which one's life is always moving into the other nine worlds. Rapture is represented by the devil of the sixth heaven. Figuratively speaking, he plays on our desires and then, as one of them is satisfied, we become overjoyed and rapturous yet heady and blind: failing to see the pitfalls and the traps that lie ahead we fall into the state of hell. In a positive sense, the function of this devil, or negative working of our own lives, is to force us to face reality. That this devil exists in the Gohonzon, illuminated by the Mystic Law, means we too can overcome the devilish force within us by chanting to the Gohonzon. The devil here is not in any sense a spirit but represents the devilish function of our own lives.

'Also present are the guardian deities of Japan: Tensho Daijin and bodhisattva Hachiman, representing the seven ranks of gods (see footnote), and all other major and minor gods in general'.
Nichiren Daishonin continues his description of the Gohonzon by referring to the guardian deities of Japan. The first one he mentions is Tensho Daijin, the traditional goddess who protects the land of Japan in Japanese folk-lore and primitive religion. In a sense, Tensho Daijin is equivalent to what St George of England stands for in Britain. Bodhisattva Hachiman who is mentioned next, 'protects' the Japanese people. Nichiren Daishonin then proceeds to mention all sorts of other traditional Japanese gods, referring to the seven ranks of heavenly gods and the five ranks of earthly gods. Nichiren Daishonin of course denied the value of worshipping these native deities of Japan directly. Instead he urged people to worship the Gohonzon. However, he included them in the Gohonzon. Rather than denying them, Nichiren Daishonin brought them into proper perspective, making them represent the various functions of nature which protect the people. All 'gods' and 'deities' are interpreted in Buddhism in this way.

Having heard all this one might be forgiven for saying, 'Well, that's fine for the Japanese, but what about us?' First of all of course, Nichiren Daishonin was born Japanese and, most important for us today, the Dai-Gohonzon which is the centre-point for our practice, is in Japan. Therefore, the protection of Japan is of universal importance. Nevertheless we find that we who live elsewhere are not to be forgotten. Although they are not mentioned in this particular passage, two other great forces or gods of the universe are represented on the Gohonzon by the names Bonten and Taishaku.

FOOTNOTE Gods. Defined in theistic religions as transcendental beings which exist apart from man. Buddhist gods on the other hand are the protective and creative forces or functions of life, inherent in the life of man, and within the universe.

Taishaku represents protective functions and interactions within society. This same force was known in Greek history as Zeus, in Rome as Jupiter and in Britain and other countries of Europe, as the Celtic guardian Odin. Bonten is the guardian force of the spiritual life of all humanity and was known in the ancient Indian religions as Brahma. This also explains why Bonten and Taishaku are specifically mentioned in the first prayer of gongyo (see later article) each morning; when gratitude is expressed for these universal forces which work in harmony with all those who make effort to live in rhythm with the law of life embodied in the Gohonzon.

> 'As all the gods appear in their essence, so they appear in their manifestations. The hoto chapter states, "All the assembly were lifted and present in the air" . . . Illuminated by the five characters of the Mystic Law, they display the enlightened nature they inherently possess. This is the true object of worship.'

We have already considered examples in which these various gods or forces of the universe can be operative in our lives, in positive or negative ways. Forces such as the sun and the moon which are inscribed on the Gohonzon are very obvious. But there are other gods or protective forces which are not so obvious: the instinct for example, which causes you to delay going out for twenty minutes, realising later than in some way you saved yourself from having an accident in the car. These protective forces are all embodied in the Gohonzon. Thus when Nichiren Daishonin says essence he means their identity on the Gohonzon, whilst manifestation is their actual function in life.

> 'Illuminated by the five characters of the Mystic Law, they display the enlightened nature they inherently possess'.

This sounds incredible. How can it be that these characters on a piece of paper are capable of doing this? Yet if we think of other pieces of paper we begin to have a clue. We all know, for example, the difference between a banknote of high value and a banknote of small value. We can spot the difference in a flash. However, if we receive a letter we have to read it very carefully and then its contents gradually become clear to us. Only then may the letter begin to affect our lives deeply.

In the same way, through studying Nichiren Daishonin's teachings and awakening the wisdom we have within, we become alive with the qualities of the Buddha state embodied in the Gohonzon. At the same time, we develop a natural desire to change our lives so that we bring out more and more perfectly and consistently the condition of Buddha revealed by the Gohonzon. The more we practise with this desire to change, the more our lives and Nichiren Daishonin's life-state embodied in the Gohonzon become as one.

This is a gradual process. When we are practising to the Gohonzon, Nichiren Daishonin said we are actually in the state of Buddhahood or enlightenment, but we cannot yet discern it with our minds; therefore we often do not act accordingly. However, through our constant relationship with the Gohonzon, we gradually challenge and overcome the influence of negativity arising from our karma. This negativity can hide from us the Gohonzon which 'exists only within the mortal flesh of us ordinary people'[2]. If we open up our lives in this way we can begin to experience all those qualities of Buddhahood working naturally and vibrantly inside us and affecting everything that we think, speak and do.

REFERENCES

(1) 'The Real Aspect of the Gohonzon' *Major Writings* Vol. 1, Page 212

(2) As above, Page 213

On prayer

by Daisaku Ikeda

'. . . the prayer made by the votary of the *Lotus Sutra* is answered as surely as an echo comes back from the sound, a shadow follows the body, a clear pool reflects the moon, a cold mirror draws moisture to it, lodestone attracts iron, amber gathers dust, and a polished mirror reflects the shape of things.'[1]

This passage assures us that the prayers of the votary of the *Lotus Sutra* will never fail to be answered. Here we can see Nichiren Daishonin's conviction in the fact that all of the analogies he draws are of real phenomena in nature. Echoes always return to the source of a sound and a shadow always follows its body. In the same way when a person chants Nam-myoho-renge-kyo, there is always a result. Nichiren Daishonin is telling us that our body and mind start to work more vigorously in response to prayer and that our environment changes in rhythm with that revitalisation.

'The prayer made by the votary of the *Lotus Sutra*', generally speaking, means those who carry out their faith and practice in exact accordance with the teachings of Nichiren Daishonin. 'Remonstration with Hachiman' reads in part:

'As long as Buddhist scholars and their students remain unaware of this, even though they read and recite all the sutras and know the twelve types of scriptures by heart, they will find it impossible to free themselves from the sufferings of birth and death. Although their prayers may seem to produce some signs at the beginning, they can never be effective enough to be heard by heaven and earth.'[2]

No prayers of this kind can ever be effective enough to set the innermost self in such vital pulsation that it can reverberate throughout the universe. The prayer of the votary of the *Lotus Sutra*, however, does resound through heaven and earth and leads to exactly the effect prayed for.

Prayer is by no means idealistic. Contemporaries who regard science as omnipotent may tend to negate the invisible aspects of human life and put prayer in the category of idealism. But so long as you only take a materialistic viewpoint of things, man to man and man to matter relations will for the most part be brought down to the level of chaos and coincidence. The penetrating wisdom of Buddhism, however, sees the Law of human life within supposed chaos and discovers that deeper force which supports and moves all phenomena.

Nichiren Daishonin states, 'It is because life does not go beyond the single moment of thought that the Buddha expounds the benefits of feeling joy to hear the Law for even a moment'.[3] As revealed here, the most important concern is that awareness, which wells up at every moment, supporting the self and giving it fundamental direction. Prayer then, is the only way to challenge ourselves at the innermost level of human existence.

Prayer is the source of correct practice and the support of perseverance in action. Nothing is as fragile as action without prayer. In favourable circumstances action without prayer may seem to be full of vigour, but once confronted with a bitter setback, it will break just like a brittle old tree. Without essential control of the innermost self, one will be swept up and down helplessly by the changing currents of society.

Life never follows a straight, gradual, upward path. Sometimes you are victorious and at other times you are defeated. Real life follows a path with many twists and turns, and as you go on, you make a milestone of growth at each step. Prayer is the thing which acts like a strong spring throughout the whole process, to enable you to persevere when you are defeated and keep you from getting too proud when you win. This is why no one is stronger than a person who seriously prays. All the more so with us, since our prayers are neither expressions of weakness and resignation, nor the fanatical kind of prayers which result from self-righteous dogmatism.

We do not pray for the protection of gods and Buddhas who stand above and control men. Rather, the intensified spiritual force of life which forms our strong prayers reveals itself as the power of faith and the power of practice. These two powers induce the power of the Buddha and the power of the Law to function within us. The initiative for the whole process rests with each individual from beginning to end.

Prayer is something which causes a change in the depths of a human heart. And the change which takes place in the depths of one person, although it may be invisible, is never confined to one individual. No more so can the change in one community ever be confined to that one community. It inevitably produces a wave of reformation which extends to other communities; in the same way that one wave creates many others. What I want to emphasise is that the force which initiates such a chain of reformation is the change which takes place in the heart of one individual. This shows the profound significance of what we mean when we say that Buddhism is reason. Nichiren Daishonin uses the words sound, body, a clear pool, etc . . ., to stand as a metaphor for prayer. And he uses the words echo, shadow, reflected moon, etc, to indicate the way prayers are answered; as naturally as can be. Just as these laws of nature reveal, the prayers of the votary of the *Lotus Sutra* are sure to be answered because they are a manifestation of the Law of life.

Nothing could be further from arrogance and conceit than these prayers. The noble figure you make when you sit upright and chant Nam-myoho-renge-kyo to the Gohonzon vividly expresses the modest spirit to strive to overcome your attachment to your shallow wisdom and meagre experience so that you can become one with the fundamental rhythm of the universe. That is, you strive to unite with the same Law of human life that the Buddha discovered with his wisdom.

You neither deprecate yourself nor become a slave to conceit, but instead you enfold all of your activities within one concentrated prayer, and while recharging the energy in your life, you prepare for a great surge of growth in the next stage. This is the healthiest and most fulfilled form of human life possible.

What we must do therefore is to grapple with all of our problems in life and at the same time pray deeply to the Gohonzon for their solution. Continuous and strenuous prayers at each new juncture and the consecutive results thereby obtained have always been the driving force of each individual human revolution.

It is vital for you to offer prayers. Everything begins from there. Unless you actually make those prayers and set your life into vivid activity, no matter how beautiful a speech you make, or how sublime a theory you may develop, it will merely be idealistic and illusory.

Prayers in Buddhism, however, never end with the mere act of prayer; they include the action one takes to realise them. It is just like an arrow, first charged with overflowing vitality, and then shot from a bow. Prayer without action is idealism, and action without prayer is futile.

A great prayer comes from a great sense of responsibility. True prayer will never grow out of an irresponsible or nonchalant attitude toward one's job, daily life or one's existence itself. Those who take responsibility for everything they are involved in and seriously grapple to improve it will develop a strong mind for their prayers.

REFERENCES
(1) 'On Prayer' *Japanese Collection* page 1347
(2) 'Remonstration with Hachiman' *Japanese Collection* page 577
(3) 'Jimyohokke Mondo Sho' *Japanese Collection* page 466

Changing karma

by Akemi Baynes

In the natural rhythm of life, the effects of bad karma from the past appear one by one in future lifetimes, but when we practise Buddhism, all the effects of past bad karma will appear in this lifetime, but in a much alleviated form. Some people think that the Buddhist principle of 'changing one's heavy karma and receiving its effect lightly' means that the effects of our past actions will become negligible or disappear without result, but this is not so. In 'The Opening of the Eyes', Nichiren Daishonin says,
> 'When iron is heated, if it is not strenuously forged, the impurities in it will not become apparent. Only when it is subjected to the tempering process again and again will the flaws appear.'[1]

To strengthen iron it needs to be tempered again and again. Each time more flaws appear until in the end the steel is flawless. Likewise, the bad karma in our lives will all gradually appear in exact proportion to the ever increasing power of our faith and practice to overcome it. There is therefore no such thing as karma being revealed which we do not have the power to overcome. Through practice, our life-force becomes stronger and we become wiser, so that step by step we are able to overcome the negative effects of all our unfortunate karma and create an indestructible, happy life. This process can be illustrated as follows. It is very hard for a six-year-old child to carry a ten pound bag up a high mountain. But for a healthy young man it is no problem at all. He can even enjoy the view as he climbs the mountain.

In order to change our karma and attain Buddhahood it is necessary to practise courageously. Life is eternal and we should aim at the great purpose of Buddhahood and Kosen rufu (see footnote), never being swayed by karma, suffering or desires. In 'Letter to the Brothers', Nichiren Daishonin quotes the *Nirvana Sutra*,
> 'By suffering sudden death, torture, slander or humiliation, beatings with a whip or rod, imprisonment, starvation,

---

FOOTNOTE. *Kosen rufu. Literally means to teach and spread widely. To secure lasting peace and happiness for all mankind through the propagation of Nichiren Daishonin's Buddhism. See later article 'Working for Peace'. It is a society in which individuals can develop their creativity without limitations; requiring as its foundation the individual struggle to reveal the Buddha state, the fundamental power to create value moment by moment.*

adversity or the relatively minor hardships of this lifetime, he will not have to fall into hell.'[2]
We may not place the above description into the category of relatively minor hardships, but we must remember what the world was like in Nichiren Daishonin's time. We can understand this if we have seen any samurai films. Nowadays these kinds of suffering are not so common in our country, but we suffer greatly from other things such as financial difficulty, divorce, pollution, fear of war and mental problems. These are our karmic retribution. Also, even though the sufferings quoted above seem very heavy, even death, if it means overcoming very heavy karma, is indeed a 'relatively minor hardship' in terms of eternal life. Once we understand the eternity of life, we can feel great joy that we are overcoming our bad karma in this lifetime. We come to understand how great and powerful Nichiren Daishonin's Buddhism is. Because we understand the eternity of life in our hearts, we can advance strongly without fear, and without being unduly swayed by whether we feel happy or sad at each moment.

In the past, many religions and philosophies have tackled the question of karma or fate. However, only Nichiren Daishonin's Buddhism has been able to explain clearly and surely the cause of karma and how to overcome it through the practice which he taught. Karma comes from the Sanskrit word *karman*, meaning actions of all kinds; physical, verbal and mental. It gradually came to mean the new set of conditions formed in a person's life through those three kinds of action.

Karma is thus formed each moment as we think, speak and act. In his writing called 'The Entity of the Mystic Law', Nichiren Daishonin explains how it is that we can change our karma through practising Nam-myoho-renge-kyo to the Gohonzon:

'. . . the Buddha discovered a Mystic Law which simultaneously contains cause and effect, and designated it as Myoho-renge. The single Law of Myoho-renge is perfectly endowed with all phenomena in the universe. Therefore, those who practise this Law simultaneously acquire the cause and effect of Buddhahood.'[3]

And in 'Lessening the Karmic Retribution', Nichiren Daishonin says:

'If one's heavy karma from the past is not expiated within this lifetime, he must undergo the sufferings of hell in the future, but if he experiences extreme hardship in this life, the sufferings of hell will vanish instantly.'[4]

The greatest benefit of all is to attain Buddhahood. This is the aim of our life and practice. Buddhahood means to realise eternal happiness. Our life is not limited to this world, it continues eternally. Attaining Buddahood in this lifetime means that we will always be full of strong life-force, have a strong sense of mission, have the freedom to achieve our aims and have great good fortune. With the Buddhism of Nichiren Daishonin we can have this kind of life continuously for thousands and thousands of lifetimes.

REFERENCES

(1) 'The Opening of the Eyes (11) *Major Writings* Vol. 2, page 202

(2) Quoted in 'Letter to the Brothers' *Major Writings* Vol. 1, page 137/8

(3) 'The Entity of the Mystic Law' *Japanese Collection* page 513

(4) 'Lessening the Karmic Retribution' *Major Writings* Vol. 1, page 17

Daily practice: Gongyo

by Dick Causton

Gongyo! For me the very word is vibrant, creating a feeling of anticipation, of a challenge which must be taken up and won. *Gon* can be translated as assiduous, eager, challenging or persistent and *gyo* means practice. Gongyo in other words, is an assiduous or challenging practice which involves doing battle daily with negative and destructive tendencies inherent in human life, which are the source of all unhappiness and despair.

In terms of the law of causality, the practice of gongyo and the pure effort which it involves is the cause to purify and elevate human life to its highest state, Buddhahood. Gongyo brings our lives into rhythm and balance with the essentially creative, dynamic yet harmonious life-force of the universe. As we struggle for a few weeks to learn to do gongyo, we are plumbing into the depths of our lives to tap and release the life-force, wisdom and compassion of the Buddha state. Thereafter, our morning and evening gongyo keeps our lives pure and free from the clutter of emotional experiences and environmental pressures of the hours in between.

Gongyo is indeed unique, and could have been devised only through the wisdom of the Buddha. It is the perfect practice, neither so difficult that it cannot be fitted into anyone's daily life-style, nor so easy that it ceases to be a weapon powerful enough to overcome the negative or devilish forces which can be so self-destructive; blocking the path to happiness and enlightenment. It is down this path that the daily practice of gongyo unfailingly leads us.

In his writings, Nichiren Daishonin exhorts us to recite the two key chapters of the *Lotus Sutra*, the second (hoben chapter) and sixteenth (juryo chapter). These two chapters contain the essence of the entire twenty-eight chapters of the sutra. Further, Nichiren Daishonin points out in his writings that, since the *Lotus Sutra* was acknowledged by Shakyamuni Buddha to be his supreme teaching, containing in itself all his previous teachings, by reciting the hoben and juryo chapters, we are embracing all the 80,000 or so teachings of Buddhism. Therefore it is our precise, rhythmic and determined recitation of these two chapters in gongyo involving mental, verbal and physical effort that begins to purify all the layers of our consciousness until we plumb Buddhahood in the depths of our lives.

This practice, followed by chanting Nam-myoho-renge-kyo polishes and purifies us, so that the life-force of Buddhahood can flow without

contamination, into every part of our spiritual and physical being.
This process of purifying our lives is enhanced through a sequence of five silent prayers. These are known in Japanese as *go kannenmon*, meaning passages for profound prayers. Each recitation of the sutra is followed by a silent prayer, five in the morning and three in the evening. The first, second and third prayers express our profound gratitude in various forms. In the fourth prayer we refresh our determination to give in return, by achieving our own self-reformation through the practice, and by giving happiness to others. Finally, in the fifth prayer we express our concern for the deceased and pray for their future happiness in terms of eternal life. We conclude with a prayer for the peace of this world and the entire universe. The process of purification having been completed, we can then begin the basic practice of chanting Nam-myoho-renge-kyo to our heart's content; causing the pure life-force of Buddhahood, combined with our strong wishes and determination, to flood into every part of our being and radiate outwards into the furthest extremities of our environment. To use an analogy, the primary practice of chanting Nam-myoho-renge-kyo is like water which we must use to wash ourselves, whilst the auxiliary practice of reciting the sutra is equivalent to soap. Without soap, it is very difficult to wash effectively.

The fruits of gongyo are quickly evident to all who practise it, even in the very first weeks of doing so. We begin to discover that 'no prayer goes unanswered' in that they always lead us to happiness and that good fortune wells up from the depths of our lives, even without our seeking it. Furthermore, we find that if we make the effort to do a vibrant and meaningful gongyo, we have successfully challenged our negative tendencies and won as our reward, an equally vibrant and meaningful day.

Citing T'ien T'ai's *Maka Shikan*, Nichiren Daishonin warns us that:
'As practice progresses and understanding grows, the three obstacles and four devils (see footnote) emerge, vying with one another to interfere'[1].

He also says:
'Were it not for these, there would be no way of knowing that this is the true teaching'[1].

In other words, the innate power of gongyo to elevate our life condition is amply proved by the negative reaction which occurs whenever we contemplate doing it! This may take many different forms such as deciding to go to sleep again or insisting on having another cup of coffee which we do not

---

FOOTNOTE. *The three obstacles and four devils. A way of classifying various obstacles to the practice of Buddhism. Obstacles are generally something or someone standing in the way of one's practice. Devils refer to one's own negativity which may be a barrier to practice. The three obstacles and four devils arise naturally to obstruct the attainment of Buddhahood. Their positive function is to point out our specific weak points; to show us precisely what makes us suffer so that we can overcome them.*

really want. This reaction is indeed the signal of the beginning of the battle for that day, and it is important to recognise that this relatively minor resistance is nothing other than the devilish force of life girding itself for the real fight to come. Our challenging attitude towards such attempts to impede us in advancing our lives is summed up in an inspiring passage from the sixteenth chapter of the *Lotus Sutra* which we recite in every gongyo:

> *Isshin yokken butsu fuji shaku shinmyo*
> 'They single-mindedly desire to see the Buddha and do not begrudge their lives.'

It should be mentioned at this point that, whilst to understand and remember the meaning of certain passages from the sutra can be inspirational, it is not essential in order to gain full benefit from the practice. In the light of the law of cause and effect, the vital point is to make effort to be clear, precise and rhythmic when reciting it. In other words, it is by no means solely a mental exercise.

Nichiren Daishonin wrote, 'When you bow to the mirror, the image in the mirror bows to you'[2], referring to the great Buddhist principle, the inseparability of man and his environment; ie one's environment always reflects back one's own life condition. Thus anger reflects anger, hell reflects hell and Buddhahood reflects Buddhahood. It is the twice daily ceremony of gongyo which ensures that our environment reflects the Buddha state which wells up in our lives through this perfect practice. Because of this we realise, to an ever increasing degree, that our environment is working in harmony with the wishes we express as we chant, instead of against us. Nichiren Daishonin states:

> 'The common mortal himself is the Buddha when he single-mindedly chants Nam-myoho-renge-kyo with strong faith. This is how he attains enlightenment naturally without discarding his life as a common mortal.'[3]

Faith in Nichiren Daishonin's Buddhism should always be manifested in action, the action of doing gongyo and teaching others to find happiness and fulfillment. Through reciting the sutra, concentrating on the silent prayers, and chanting Nam-myoho-renge-kyo, we can purify our lives. Through praising and showing our gratitude to the Mystic Law, the Law of life, in our daily practice, we bring untold benefit, not only for ourselves but for our environment; for our family; society and the land in which we live. In this connection, the great Buddhist teacher Dengyo (also known as Saicho, 767–822 AD) wrote:

> 'Because slandering voices are raised throughout the land, countless thousands perish: but if a single family diligently praises the true teachings, the seven disasters will abate.'[4]

During gongyo one truly feels one with the boundless universe, a soaring sense

of freedom and expansion unrestricted by time or space, which is yet rooted in this earth and subsequently overflows into our ordinary, very human, daily lives. It was with this in mind that Daisaku Ikeda wrote:
'The emergence of Buddhahood from within your own life bursts the bonds of the ego, breaks the shackles of human destiny and proclaims the total liberation of life. As we continue the practice of gongyo, our lives become fixed in the world of enlightenment; and at that time, we can establish an indestructible happiness that transcends the cycle of life and death. In order to build an unyielding bulwark to withstand the storms of life, we have no choice but to practise gongyo.'[5]

Just as Shakyamuni predicted almost 3,000 years ago, Nichiren Daishonin, through his enlightenment, has handed down to us the practice which possesses the limitless power necessary to steer a steady course towards absolute happiness and fulfillment in this lifetime, even in this chaotic age.

REFERENCES

(1) 'Letter to the Brothers' *Major Writings* Vol. 1, page 145

(2) Quoted in Daisaku Ikeda 'Gongyo' *Seikyo Times* July 1981, page 22

(3) 'Honninnmyo Sho' *Japanese Collection* page 872

(4) Quoted in Daisaku Ikeda 'Gongyo' *Seikyo Times* July 1981 page 21

(5) As above page 22

Part 3.
Origins and Evolution

Springing from the earth

Springing from the Earth

Traveller!
where have you come from?
where are you going?

The moon has set
the sun not yet risen
in the chaos before dawn
searching for the light
I press onward

To drive back the dark clouds of the mind
I seek the great tree unshaken by the storm —
will I spring up from the great earth of life?

Daisaku Ikeda

Cosmos, religion, culture

by Daisaku Ikeda

Developed by Shakyamuni in India, Buddhism passed into other parts of Asia where it invariably had a vitalising effect on the minds of men. However in both India and China, once its peak and glory was passed, Buddhism quickly declined, until today it can be considered dead in both countries. I seriously doubt whether the Buddhism existing today in such South-East Asian countries as Thailand, Burma and Kampuchea, is in consonance with the true spirit of the highest teachings of Buddhism, because to be alive a religion must be an object of earnest faith, giving people strength and wisdom to challenge the sufferings they face in everyday life. Even religions that have inspired the creation of societies and cultures turn into fetters once they become rigid, since human beings must live in the constantly changing flow of history.

In a broad sense, civilisation consists of the things that man has developed in order to deal with and overcome the problems of suffering. Though nature gives birth to and sustains all forms of life, including man, it is capricious. While in some times and places it allows people to enjoy the good things of life, at others it is barren and cold, and withholds nourishment; thus compelling people to die of hunger or illness.

To avoid being completely at the mercy of nature's changing moods, man has used his intelligence to discover and develop the use of fire, food preparation and storage, housing, clothing, medical techniques and medicaments, and other things too numerous to list here. Certainly one of the greatest steps in this direction was the discovery and spread of agricultural methods. As a consequence of such discoveries and inventions, man has been freed from the need to wait for the blessings of nature and has become capable of deliberately cultivating the natural environment.

Because of developments in agriculture and other technical skills, human lifestyles have fundamentally changed. Technology and various operational achievements have required large-scale and complicated organisations, which in turn gave rise to the relations between ruler and ruled and to an intensified awareness of the differences among the social classes. In other words, artificial developments brought into being the kind of sufferings which do not exist in the natural order of things. This effect has not been limited to external matters, for the advances of civilisation have greatly intensified the suffering which plagues man's inner world. Though civilisation has undeniably developed the power to prevent starvation, death from cold, and illness which frequently accompanied natural disasters in the distant past, death in one form or another must still come to every man. Medical science can eradicate some kinds of sickness but it cannot eliminate death. Nor have any of the other blessings of civilisation been able to change human destiny.

Nonetheless, as civilisation has advanced, a hope that death can somehow be escaped has developed in the human mind. Man has lost the ability to accept death calmly as an inevitable event since people began using their intelligence in ways extending beyond the present and searching for explanation of the eternal. It was not, however, until civilisation attempted to prove that there may be something effective against mortality, that the old fear of death took the form of tenacious attachment to life.

Primitive peoples of the distant past buried their dead with some kind of ceremony. Though this may not represent actual resistance to death, it does indicate a belief that life exists after death.

With advances in civilisation, resistance against death became more remarkable. The pharaohs of Egypt constructed immense pyramids believing this would guarantee an afterlife, and the emperors of China used their great power and authority in far-ranging searches for an elixir of life. It seems likely, however, that the majority of the ordinary people in those times accepted death almost without question, since they had little reason to love their existence. But as the blessings of civilisation finally reached them too, they developed an attachment to the idea of living, and resistance to death became universal. Today, death is only indirectly experienced in the ordinary household because many people die in hospitals or some other kind of institution.

Civilisation has enabled man to turn his eyes away from death, but has not succeeded in removing the fact of dying. The inevitability of death is bound up with life. Civilisation has made life more comfortable. It has to some extent guaranteed the material essentials of life, but alone, such a guarantee is not enough, because, as his intelligence has developed, man has been compelled to examine himself more objectively. The significance of his existence has thus become an issue of the greatest concern.

The act of living is not in itself an ultimate goal but gains eternal meaning through a deeper, universal purpose. A life without such a purpose is essentially ephemeral. The fundamental reason for religions is the desire for something that will impart an eternal meaning to life. Primitive religions typify this way of thinking. But such religions pay great attention to placating natural forces in the hope of winning the goodwill of the unknown powers believed to be behind them and thus of ensuring the good things essential to life.

The Hebrews were probably the first to claim that a single, absolute god is the source of all things in the universe and the arbiter of life, death and destiny. In establishing one fixed interpretation of life, they made a great contribution to human spiritual history. However, Buddhism has followed a course entirely different from theistic religions. The Buddhist interpretation of the universe is that all things, including life, death and destiny, in essence are the Mystic Law and that enlightenment to this Law constitutes the way of giving eternal value and significance to ephemeral life.

Buddhist truth was discovered as a result of the enlightenment experienced by Shakyamuni, who was born a prince of the Shakya tribe in ancient India and lived a life of wealth and ease throughout his youth. But being an innately sensitive and perceptive man, who thought deeply about the problems of human life and the world and who tended to seek a way of truth within himself, Shakyamuni later abandoned the splendour of his home and devoted himself to a life of religious discipline. His motivations reveal some of the characteristic features of Buddhist teachings.

According to tradition, Shakyamuni made four sorties from the four gates in the walls around Kapilavastu, his father's capital city. One day, he went out of the city from the eastern gate and encountered an old man. This caused him to reflect on the sorrow of ageing. Another day, he went out of the city by the western gate and saw a funeral procession, which caused him to reflect on the sorrow of death. On the third day, he went out by the southern gate and encountered a sick person, who brought to his mind the sorrows of illness. On the fourth day, he went out by the northern gate and saw a religious ascetic. This made him resolve to give up his home and family and devote himself to the religious life.

Though it may be no more than a legend, the story clearly reveals the inner human problems that had engrossed Shakyamuni throughout his youth. The old person, the sick person and the corpse represent the three sufferings of ageing, illness and death which no human being can escape. Shakyamuni's decision to leave home was motivated by a desire to deal with the sorrows of human existence. No matter how times change and no matter how far science and learning advance, they alone can do nothing to solve the problems of these most basic sufferings of human existence.

Upon leaving his life of ease, Shakyamuni launched on a vigorous spiritual struggle and a course of ascetic disciplines lasting, according to various sources, either six or seven years. During this time he surpassed all his fellow ascetics in difficult tests. Legends and stories relate them in some detail. But ascetic practices did not bring him enlightenment. Ultimately, he was enlightened at the outcome of a period of profound meditation as he sat under the Bodhi tree. Shakyamuni's enlightenment is the first example of the spiritual struggle in which Buddhist truth manifests itself.

The truth Shakyamuni became enlightened to was the Law, which has existed from time immemorial. It is said that Shakyamuni himself announced the existence of other Buddhas who had become aware of this truth before him, but since he was the first to affirm this truth in the course of history, he is considered the founder of Buddhism. The meaning of the word Buddha is 'the enlightened one', and the word in no way indicates divinity of the kind worshipped in theistic religions.

What then is the nature of the truth to which Shakyamuni was enlightened while meditating under the Bodhi tree? The answer to this question is to be found in the *Lotus Sutra*, which contains the most complete explanation of Shakyamuni's enlightenment.

The truth of this enlightenment was the discovery of the Law of life pervading the universe, nature, mankind and all phenomena. The Law is an eternal, indestructible truth extending throughout the entire universe, and throughout the course of past, present and future. While Shakyamuni was meditating, he experienced the essential reality of man and the world and the rhythm of constant change and creation taking place at every instant in all things in the cosmos. Nothing in the universe remains static. Human beings must progress steadily along the path of ageing to death. And, after death, the life-force manifested in the individual will be reborn to continue the cycle. The constant change in the universe is reflected in the constant generation and destruction in the world of nature and in the character of human life. All living things exist in a total interrelationship. Shakyamuni was enlightened to this and to the truth that all things are continually serving as causes and effects of changes within these interrelationships.

The cosmos referred to is explained in the *Lotus Sutra* and in the doctrine of 'three-thousand worlds in a moment of life' (see article page 38), systemised in China by Chih-i (538–972), known as the great teacher T'ien-t'ai. This doctrine holds that the entire universe is concentrated in a single human life. Therefore, a single human life is capable of influencing the entire universe. Shakyamuni discovered the wonderful truth that all phenomena and human lives are mutually related, influential and permeating. This discovery made him a Buddha. Enlightenment to the Law of life relating to the entire universe and for all eternity, solved for him problems of birth, ageing, illness and death. This simultaneously became a basis for the liberation of all humanity from suffering.

Though most ordinary people remain unaware of the Law deep within their own lives and consequently suffer the anxieties of the four kinds of suffering, the *Lotus Sutra* teaches that all beings, sentient and insentient, can manifest the state of Buddha within them and that all human beings can attain Buddahood. Whether that possibility is realised depends on whether the individual human being becomes enlightened to the eternal Law of life. There is no absolute barrier between a Buddha and an ordinary person as there is between human beings and God in Christianity. The doctrine contained in the

Lotus Sutra, to the effect that Buddhahood is inherent in all living things, is the fundamental meaning of Shakyamuni's teachings. The problem is for ordinary people to perceive the Law of life. If they fail to grasp a concrete method, Shakyamuni's enlightenment remains nothing but a theory with no power to enable human beings to overcome their present sufferings. Realising this, Shakyamuni travelled from place to place for approximately fifty years after his enlightenment teaching the truth in various ways which were adapted to the capacities of his audience. Activities of this kind earned for him the epithet 'teacher of mankind' and produced the countless teachings that have born much fruit and have continued to be a glorious part of the human heritage to the present day.

The enlightened Shakyamuni knew that human beings are confused because of their ignorance of the Law of life and because of delusions and attachments to worldly affairs. These are particularly strong when human beings regard their own existence as separate from the laws of nature, and interpret society and the world in the light of their own interests and needs. Such an interpretation is a delusion because, as Shakyamuni proved, everything in the universe is constantly changing; nothing is permanent. He further attempted to convince the people he taught, of the truth that all things in the universe are interrelated and contained within one great life-force.

The sufferings of birth, old age, illness and death result from the human misconception that the individual life is independent of all other phenomena and that the individual is in some way absolute and capable of living a totally self-oriented life. But when this attitude is abandoned in favour of the belief that the individual life is closely connected with the great universal life-force, the four sufferings can be converted into the four kingdoms of enlightenment: freedom from change, suffering, bondage and illusion. When the various sutras are read in the light of this belief, their unity in diversity becomes apparent.

Other teachings of Shakyamuni – the triple doctrine that all phenomena are impermanent, that there is no permanent self, and that nirvana is tranquillity, plus the doctrines of the void, the oneness of illusions and Buddhahood, and the unity of birth and death with nirvana – were evolved to help people understand the Law of life. But the teachings of Shakyamuni are seriously limited because they go no further than pointing out the existence of this Law of life. As long as he was alive, Shakyamuni, as an actual manifestation of the Law, was able to liberate people from sufferings.

After the death of Shakyamuni, Buddhism experienced a long period of transition from flourishing to decay, followed by revival and ruin again. Upon the death of their master, the followers of Shakyamuni felt that collecting his teachings, with the aim of passing them on in correct form to later generations, was a task of maximum importance. They abided by his parting instructions to rely only on the Law and not on persons propounding the Law. The first council held to collect the teachings, took place shortly after his death, in Rajagriha, the capital of Magadha, then a kingdom in eastern India. At this meeting, five hundred of the disciples recited his teachings one by one to determine their correctness. At the conclusion of the council, they dispersed to their native regions to carry the teachings to other peoples. The loss of their leader must have saddened these men greatly, but they overcame their personal feelings to undertake the work of propagation, which was especially difficult because of the power of the Brahmans in the India of those times. Owing to their efforts, Buddhism, concentrating on eastern India and on the leading cities in each region, soon found a place in the hearts of the people. The early disciples adhered closely to the precepts left to them by Shakyamuni and protected the Law.

About one hundred years after Shakyamuni's death in the traditionally prosperous, free-trading city of Vaishali, a schism occurred in the Buddhist Order, between a conservative group of elders who wished to observe the old precepts, and another more progressive group, who were closer to the general populace and more actively engaged in propagation. The conservative element of the Order called the second council. At this time, another group of about ten thousand followers who devoted themselves to propagation, compiled a collection of teachings that was later to become of central importance to Mahayana Buddhism.

When another century had passed, King Ashoka, the third monarch in the Maurya dynasty, became a Buddhist. The series of fourteen edicts he had carved on stones and pillars all over the country are based on the Buddhist Law. In addition, he had many reliquary towers (stupas) erected, a large number of which are today being excavated in India, Pakistan and Afghanistan. During the thirty years of his reign, Buddhism spread from eastern India throughout the subcontinent and into neighbouring countries. Laymen took part in the dedication of stupas. In the second half of the third century BC, Buddhism was active in a greater area of India and the surrounding regions than ever before in its history.

By this time, however, the Order had split into more than twenty factions. Although throughout all of them the basic teachings remained unaltered, differences of opinion had arisen in minor matters. Concerned about this state of affairs, King Ashoka called the third council which was held in his capital, Pataliputra, in order to determine the basic Law on which all the teachings rested.

When the Mauryan dynasty fell, indigenous Indian religions began to revive with the result that Buddhism went into a period of decline for a while. During this period, Buddhist scholars engaged in theoretical disputes with representatives of other religions and attempted to further knowledge of the

Law by compiling the Abhidharma collection of commentaries on the sutras (such commentaries are called *shastras*). In the latter, discipline was stressed in an attempt to study doctrines in greater detail.

At about the middle of the first century of the Christian Era, the Kushanas (called the Yueh-chih by the Chinese of the Han dynasty) invaded north-western India. Under their third monarch, Kanishka, Mahayana Buddhism enjoyed great prosperity. In the Gandhara Plain, in the vicinity of modern Peshawar, under Kushana patronage, many Buddhist buildings were erected, and the famous Gandhara style of Buddhist art came into being.

Under the Kushana dynasty, Buddhism spread beyond the realm of Indian culture to reach Central Asia and China. The Yueh-chih ultimately carried Mahayana Buddhism so far afield along the old Silk Road, that it became a unifying element among the peoples of India, China, Japan and other Asian nations. At about the same time, Theravada Buddhism (also called Hinayana Buddhism), the system favoured by the conservative elders of the order, was spreading to Sri Lanka and South-East Asia. This was the period when Buddhism truly became the religion of the Asian people.

The history of Chinese Buddhism begins with the early efforts to translate into Chinese the Buddhist classics brought into the country from Central Asia along the Silk Road by the Yueh-chih and other peoples. Between the second and twelfth centuries of the Christian era, an immense number of Buddhist classics were translated.

But, while classification of the teachings was going on, arguments among priests became so prevalent that, in spite of theoretical advances, Buddhism tended to move further and further away from the ordinary people. On some occasions, the disputes caused the Chinese Imperial power to intervene; thus threatening the Buddhists with oppression or even worse.

Chinese Buddhism reached its peak in the sixth century, when Chih-i (or T'ien-t'ai the Great) organised the religion around the *Lotus Sutra*, the Mahayana classic of paramount importance, and founded the T'ien-t'ai school of Buddhism. After this, Buddhism steadily declined until, two hundred years after Chih-i, when a Japanese priest called Saicho (also known as the great teacher Dengyo), travelled to China and brought T'ien-t'ai teachings back to Japan, where Buddhism was once again to flourish.

Among Buddhists there has long been a belief that the teachings would travel in a north-easterly direction from India, as indeed they have. I am deeply moved by the strivings and faith of the people who have enabled the word of the Buddha to survive the severe climate of the Asian continent and all the vicissitudes of time and circumstances to reach Japan. But I regret the fate Buddhism has suffered in India, China and Central Asia, where very little remains of its former influence.

Doctrinal obscurity and rigidity of discipline can be cited as reasons for the failure of Buddhism and the loss of its following among the ordinary people. Understanding the true nature of Shakyamuni's enlightenment, even by reading the *Lotus Sutra*, where it is fully explained, is not easy. Difficult concepts, metaphorical language and the immense gap between the present and the days of Shakyamuni, prevented the masses from understanding it. Instructions to study and believe the *Lotus Sutra*, and to cherish, read, recite and make commentaries on it, were scarcely applicable to the illiterate. Only the upper classes had sufficient education for this purpose. The T'ien-t'ai school's approach called for meditation (though Zen has made such meditation famous today all over the world, it actually started in connection with study of the *Lotus Sutra*), but it also demanded study and commentaries for an understanding of the theory of the 'three thousand worlds in a moment of life'. Once again, this was beyond the ability of the masses.

In reaction against the difficulties of such Buddhist teachings, the Jodo (meaning pure land) and Zen sects emerged. Both of them actually originated in China after the T'ien-t'ai school went into decline. In Japan, they quickly rose to prominence in the disturbed times following the death of Dengyo, the collapse of the old aristocracy, and the rise to power of the military classes in the twelfth century. Both sects rejected study of difficult texts and philosophical speculation. The Jodo sect, which teaches that merely calling on the name of the Buddha Amida and a fervent hope for salvation are all that is needed, spread rapidly among the ordinary people. Also inherent in this teaching is the belief in paradise after death. But the desire to reach this paradise is said to have made many people pessimistic about life. What we have said so far, however, should have proved that there is no pessimism in the true teachings of Shakyamuni, who advocated liberation from the four sufferings, and religious practices which are easy even for the uneducated masses.

Nichiren Daishonin boldly changed ways of thinking about the enlightenment of Shakyamuni, when he proclaimed that the *Lotus Sutra* is the true reason for the appearance of the Buddha in the world, and that it should be the basis of religious practice on the part of the ordinary people. While continuing to use the Japanese reading of the title given to the sutra by the famous translator Kumarajiva (344–413 AD), Nichiren Daishonin delved deeply into the meaning of the text and showed that the Law of the essential teachings of Buddhism for the latter period (the present, chaotic times when the teachings of Shakyamuni have lost validity) is not to be found in Shakyamuni's *Lotus Sutra* but in Nam-myho-renge-kyo, the Law of the eternal Buddha. In other words, Nichiren Daishonin established a new Buddhism, which he discovered as a result of his own experience. This new Buddhism encompasses all of the teachings of Shakyamuni, including of course the *Lotus Sutra*. Furthermore, Nichiren Daishonin created the mandala of Nam-myoho-renge-kyo (the Gohonzon), which is the essence of the *Lotus Sutra* as well as its title and the major object of veneration for all who believe in his Buddhism.

The mandala is not to be confused with other mandalas which make idols of Buddhas and bodhisattvas, for example, those employed in the ceremonies of the Shingon sect of esoteric Buddhism. Aware that he was himself the eternal Buddha, Nichiren Daishonin gave graphic form to his own enlightenment in this mandala. His writings say that Shakyamuni's intention by appearing in this world was to preach the *Lotus Sutra*, and that 'the soul of Nichiren is Nam-myoho-renge-kyo' and evokes in the individual human being a surge of the same life-force that filled the Buddha. Undeniably, in doing this, Nichiren Daishonin created a new living Buddhism that simultaneously manifests the fundamental Law and provides ordinary people with a teaching that can be easily understood and practised.

The heritage of the Law

by Dick Causton

The Buddhist priest who later called himself Nichiren, meaning Sun Lotus, was born on 16th February 1222 in a village called Kominato, in Chiba Prefecture in Japan. Although he was born to a fisherman's family, he must have been an unusually bright and intelligent boy, for at the age of twelve he was sent to enter his local temple for his general education and to study Buddhism. This temple, called Seicho-ji, high upon Mount Kiyosumi, was representative of the state of Buddhism throughout Japan at that time. That is to say, although it had originally been a centre of learning for the Tendai sect (which based its study and practice mainly on the *Lotus Sutra* in accordance with the teachings of T'ien-t'ai), it had later absorbed a great deal of the esoteric beliefs and mystic rituals of the Shingon sect. It also later absorbed the teachings of the Jodo (or pure land) sect, with its reliance on the worship of a mythical Buddha called Amida in order to lead one to a form of paradise or pure land after death.

Nichiren Daishonin entered the priesthood at sixteen, and by the time he was eighteen had left Seicho-ji on the first of a series of journeys to study at the most important Buddhist centres of learning in Japan. This was to totally occupy his time for the next thirteen years. We know now, from his theses and letters (more than four hundred of which are still preserved in their original form), that these expeditions to study all the Buddhist teachings which existed in Japan, had a most specific purpose. For us to begin to understand this, it is necessary to look briefly at the times into which Nichiren Daishonin had been born.

The first half of the 13th century in mediaeval Japan was a period of unprecedented misery for the people. For more than forty years the country was struck by a series of natural disasters of an intensity, never before or since, experienced. Earthquakes, typhoons, floods, droughts, famines and widespread epidemics occurred one after another, reaching a peak in the years 1256 to 1259. At the same time members of the ruling clan, who had wrested power from the emperors in the previous century, were still struggling amongst themselves for the supreme position of authority and seeking ways to establish an iron grip on the people, reaching out to every corner of Japan. Meanwhile, from across the Japan Sea came a stream of rumours that the great Mongol Empire, which in 1259 had completed the subjugation of Korea under

Khubilai Khan, would next turn their attention to conquering Japan.

With this background it is not difficult to visualise the state of tension and fear which filled the hearts of the people under the constant threat of fatal sickness or violent death. Nichiren Daishonin described this situation graphically in a thesis he wrote in 1260 to the retired regent Hojo Tokiyori, who was at that time the most powerful man in Japan. The opening paragraph reads:

> 'In recent years, there are unusual disturbances in the heavens, strange occurrences on earth, famine and pestilence, all affecting every corner of the empire and spreading thoughout the land. Oxen and horses lie dead in the streets, the bones of the stricken crowd the highways. Over half the population has already been carried off by death, and in every family someone grieves'.[1]

Even as a very young man, Nichiren Daishonin had been struck by the fact that the chaotic state of life and the terrible sufferings of the people, must have relevance to the confusion which existed in the practice of religion in Japan at that time. In particular, he believed that the true teachings propounded approximately 2,000 years previously by Shakyamuni had become distorted. Thus, the purpose of his journeys and intense periods of study over these thirteen years was to discover how, and in what way, the various sects had veered from the true way, distorting Shakyamuni's teachings and, as a result, weakening the power of religion for the good of mankind and his environment.

At this point we should start to examine the nature of Nichiren Daishonin's enlightenment. To do this we must first turn to the *Lotus Sutra*, expounded, it is believed, in the last eight years of Shakyamuni's life-time and known in Sanskrit as the *Saddharma Pundarika Sutram*.

Shakyamuni clearly declared the supremacy of the *Lotus Sutra* over all his previous teachings, stating in the 10th chapter for example, that:

> 'Of all my teachings and all my sutras, the *Lotus Sutra* is supreme. Among all the sutras I have preached, now preach and will preach, this *Lotus Sutra* is the most difficult to understand.'[2]

Again, in the *Muryogi Sutra*, the *Sutra of Infinite Meaning*, which is the prologue of the *Lotus Sutra* he said:

> 'In these more than forty years, I have not yet revealed the truth'.[3]

Whilst in the 2nd or hoben chapter Shakyamuni said,

> 'Honestly discarding the provisional teachings, I will expound the supreme Law'.[4]

Thus Shakyamuni clearly indicated in these and many other passages, that the *Lotus Sutra* was supreme, since it contained within it the essential truth from which the partial truths of all his previous teachings were derived. Hence these previous, or provisional teachings as he called them, should now be discarded.

Nevertheless, later in the *Lotus Sutra* he also began to make it clear that the teaching of the Mystic Law, although supreme, was not only for his time but was specifically for the people of the latter period of the Law, that evil age which, according to the *Daijuku* or *Mahasanghata Sutra*, would begin about 2,000 years after Shakyamuni's death. While scholars may still argue about the year and even the century, of Shakyamuni's death, there can be no doubt, for more reasons than one, that we today have all been born into this troubled age. For example, in the 17th chapter of the *Lotus Sutra* it states that good medicine (a reference to the story of the excellent physician in the preceding 16th chapter), is left for 'those of the evil filled latter day of the Law' [5]; whilst the 23rd chapter states:

'In the fifth five hundred years after my death, accomplish world-wide Kosen rufu and never allow its flow to cease.'[6]

This is a reference to the five half-millennia expounded in the *Daijuku Sutra*, by means of which Shakyamuni predicted that during the first two half-millennia after his death, his pure law would remain efficacious for the people. In the third and fourth half-millenia, it would become formalised and ritualised, gradually losing its power to help mankind, finally reaching its nadir in the latter period of the Law when it would be replaced by the ultimate truth of the *Lotus Sutra*.

What was this ultimate truth? Nichiren Daishonin insisted that it is indicated in two chapters of the *Lotus Sutra*, namely the 2nd (hoben) chapter and the 16th (juryo) chapter. In the former, which belongs to the theoretical teachings, Shakyamuni made the astounding revelation to those who had become accustomed to regarding him as almost super-human, that the Buddha nature is inherent in all common mortals; whilst in the 16th chapter, which belongs to the essential teachings, he gave his experience of Buddhahood: that he had not become enlightened for the first time in northern India under the bodhi tree, but had become so countless aeons ago in the far distant past, having practised the bodhisattva austerities.

From Nichiren Daishonin's point of view and for those who follow his teachings, it is an important fact that never once in the *Lotus Sutra* does Shakyamuni explain how he attained enlightenment. What was the key that opened his life to the Law? Nevertheless, from the 11th to the 22nd chapters of the *Lotus Sutra*, he proceeded to give his experience of enlightenment and how his revelation of the Law in the *Lotus Sutra* would be transmitted over the centuries to the people of the latter period of the Law. This he did by means of an elaborate and most spectacular allegory, rather similar to a contemporary space drama, known as the treasure tower and the ceremony in the air. Through this story he told his disciples (who had gathered to listen to the *Lotus*

Sutra and who had volunteered to propagate the Mystic Law in the age we now live in), that they would never be able to cope with the obstacles and difficulties to be encountered in this 'dreaded age'. Instead the Mystic Law would be propagated by countless people who would rise up amidst the 'three poisons' (ie anger, greed and ignorance or stupidity) of that evil age and who would follow the path of the bodhisattvas of the earth. These people would be like lotus flowers, revealing perfect white blooms from roots sunk in the muddy swamp, the actuality of daily life. For this reason, whilst Shakyamuni's Buddhism is known as the Buddhism of the harvest, which reveals only his enlightenment, but not the way to reach it, the Buddhism of the age we live in is the Buddhism of the sowing, establishing the way for all people to attain enlightenment in a single lifetime.

This, briefly, is the historical and literary validation surrounding Nichiren Daishonin's founding of true Buddhism. It remained for him to translate the essence of his enlightenment into a practical teaching suitable for ordinary people, not only of his own time but far into the future of the latter period of the Law, which is said to last for ten thousand years and more into eternity. Furthermore the aim of this practice could not be anything less than it should unfailingly lead those who devote themselves to it, to Buddhahood in a single life-time.

The title of any Buddhist sutra contains within itself the essence of the teaching expounded in that sutra. Following this principle, Nichiren Daishonin knew that the title of the *Lotus Sutra*, which, translated into Chinese and using the Japanese pronounciation for the characters, is Myoho-renge-kyo, contained within it the heart of the teaching and was in itself the enlightenment of all Buddhas. Indeed this was why Shakyamuni had said, 'Honestly discarding previous teachings' and 'I have not yet revealed the truth'. Myoho-renge-kyo was indeed the creative force of life itself; the life-force at the heart of every living thing including of course, human beings and all phenomena in the universe. Myoho-renge-kyo, in other words, was the pulsating, vibrating rhythm of life itself. By recognising that Myoho-renge-kyo was the essence of their lives, human beings could achieve harmony at last, not only with the environment surrounding them, but also, most importantly, with themselves. Through this harmony, people would be able to live creative, happy, fulfilling lives which would essentially be valuable and consistent with the needs, not only of the immediate environment, but also of the universe as a whole. As will be explained later however, Myoho-renge-kyo itself is theory. Even after Shakyamuni had expounded it, people found it very difficult to realise in their daily lives. This is why Nichiren Daishonin embodied it in the form of the Gohonzon and thus established the way to manifest the truth of Myoho-renge-kyo in our lives now. On 28th April 1253, at Seicho-ji Temple, Nichiren Daishonin declared the first of the three great secret laws (secret in the sense that they had always existed yet had not been revealed by the Buddha). This was, that to be happy man should devote his whole life to maintaining rhythm with the Law of life itself by chanting Nam-myoho-renge-kyo, as a daily invocation, the syllable *Nam*, meaning to devote oneself. Through this, we can derive the life-force of Buddhahood from Myoho-renge-kyo.

This declaration became a direct challenge to the established Buddhist sects of the time, (whose doctrines were based on the provisional teachings of Shakyamuni) and indeed, to the ruling authorities who sponsored them. This resulted in Nichiren Daishonin having to endure relentless persecutions throughout most of his life-time. There were many attempts on his life, including an attempt to execute him; he was exiled twice and on other occasions beaten. (These events are all recorded in his writings.) Yet he was able to endure all this joyfully, continuing to fulfill his mission, writing, teaching and ultimately inscribing the Gohonzon. This buoyancy, despite all opposition, was reinforced by his understanding that his persecutions were exactly fulfilling the predictions made by Shakyamuni in the 13th chapter of the *Lotus Sutra*, concerning the persecutions the votary of the *Lotus Sutra* would suffer in spreading the Mystic Law in the latter period. It is interesting to read his account of one of the lesser persecutions in a writing called 'Persecution by Sword and Staff':

> 'As I mentioned before, I was attacked by the sword at Komatsubara in Tojo and later at Tatsunokuch. No one else has been thus assaulted for the sake of the *Lotus Sutra* even once, but I, Nichiren, have been so assaulted twice . . . As for being attacked with staves, I have already been struck in the face by Shofu-bo with the scroll of the fifth volume of the *Lotus Sutra*. Strangely enough, it is precisely that volume which carries the prediction that the votaries of the *Lotus Sutra* will be attacked with staves. Shofu-bo hit me before dozens of people, and though I knew it was for the sake of the *Lotus Sutra*, being human, I felt miserable and ashamed. Had I had the strength, I would have wrested the weapon from his hand and trampled it to pieces, except that it was in fact the scroll of the fifth volume of the *Lotus Sutra*'. (Note: at the time of Nichiren Daishonin, the 13th chapter was in the 5th volume of the *Lotus Sutra*.)

Twenty-seven years after declaring Nam-myoho-renge-kyo, having gradually taught his disciples and followers to embrace this practice and, seeing that they could protect the orthodox flow of true Buddhism, he established the second of the three great secret laws. On 12th October 1279, he inscribed the object of devotion, a great mandala, known as the Dai-Gohonzon, which is enshrined to this day in the head temple of Nichiren Shoshu at Taiseki-ji, at the foot of Mount Fuji in Japan.

When he inscribed the Gohonzon, Nichiren Daishonin said, 'I, Nichiren, have inscribed my life in ink'. That is to say, the object of devotion is a representation in Chinese (and two Sanskrit) characters of Nichiren Daishonin's life which was one with the Law, in the state of Buddhahood. Many of the characters on the Gohonzon express fully the true meaning and intent of the treasure tower and ceremony in the air which Shakyamuni had used allegorically in the Lotus Sutra, to transmit his experience of enlightenment, or of being one with the Law in the Buddha state. This is what Nichiren Daishonin is referring to when he says:

'. . . the object of worship which perfectly depicts Shakyamuni in the treasure tower and all the other Buddhas who were present, as accurately as the print matches the woodblock.'[8]

In this sense the Gohonzon inscribed by Nichiren Daishonin incorporates documentary proof of the flow of Buddhism through the ages from the earlier Buddhism of Shakyamuni. However, the Gohonzon itself, together with the invocation of Nam-myoho-renge-kyo, are the direct result of the enlightenment of Nichiren Daishonin, providing the foundation for the Buddhism of this age and onwards into eternity. This is shown on the Gohonzon by the bold characters running down its centre, which signify the oneness of the Law of Nam-myoho-renge-kyo and the person, Nichiren.

Through the daily practice of chanting Nam-myoho-renge-kyo to the Gohonzon, we see, as if in a mirror, what our own lives can be like. And most importantly, from this arises the determination to change ourselves through the power of this practice, until our life state can actually match the life state of the Gohonzon. Thus Nichiren Daishonin referred to the Gohonzon as *kanjin no honzon*; the object of devotion for attaining enlightenment through observing the truth of one's life.

Nichiren Daishonin died in 1282, three years after inscribing the Dai-Gohonzon which was the fulfillment of the whole purpose of his life. It remained for his followers to achieve his will and testament by fulfilling the third great secret Law, which was to establish the *kaidan*, or ultimate high sanctuary for the Dai-Gohonzon at the foot of Mount Fuji at the time of Kosen rufu. The Dai-Gohonzon is now enshrined in the Sho Hondo, (grand main temple), in the grounds of the head temple of Nichiren Shoshu at Taiseki-ji. The ceremony of worshipping the Dai-Gohonzon is attended almost daily by tens of thousands of Nichiren Shoshu members, not only from Japan, but also from all over the world. Indeed, the Dai-Gohonzon was inscribed as the prime point for all human beings to attain Buddhahood; their highest life state. This prime point is the means for people to transform all forms of inherent negativity which ultimately cause war and violence, as well as the other evils which afflict the world. These have their source in the hearts and minds of men and women.

The Sho Hondo and the ever-increasing numbers of people from more than 100 countries who go to express their devotion to the Dai-Gohonzon are establishing the essential conditions for peace in the world; through the transformation taking place in the depths of an ever growing number of human beings' lives. These followers of Nichiren Daishonin are indeed the followers of the way of the bodhisattvas of the earth whose appearance is predicted in the *Lotus Sutra*, and who rise up from the murky swamp of our present age, teaching others of the power of the Gohonzon. They too, can then transform their lives and blossom like lotus flowers, not in the rarefied atmosphere of some mountain top, like some of the saints and sages of old, but in their ordinary daily lives and in any and every field of society.

REFERENCES

(1) 'Rissho Ankoku Ron' *Major Writings* Vol. 2, page 3

(2) *Lotus Sutra* Chapter 10

(3) Quoted in 'The Opening of the Eyes' (1) *Major Writings* Vol. 2, page 101

(4) As above, page 102

(5) *Lotus Sutra* Chapter 17

(6) *Lotus Sutra* Chapter 23

(7) 'Persecution by Sword and Staff' *Major Writings* Vol. 2, page 304

(8) The Real Aspect of the Gohonzon *Major Writings* Vol. 1, page 212

The growth of Nichiren Shoshu Buddhism

by Mike Eggleton

During the more than seven hundred years since the founding of Nichiren Daishonin's Buddhism in 1253, its teachings and doctrines have been protected and handed down in absolute purity by sixty-seven successive high priests.

Throughout this long period, effort was made to spread Nichiren Shoshu in Japan, but the effect was always limited by the restriction on religious freedom in the country. Absolute freedom of religion was only finally established by the American occupation forces after the ending of the second world war. It was also from the end of the war, that the lay society of Nichiren Shoshu, which later called itself Soka Gakkai (literally, 'society for the creation of value') began to exhibit its phenomenal growth. Over the centuries, the only type of lay organisation permitted had been small groups centred around local temples. After the war, it was possible for the first time to establish a body with a nationwide membership.

From 1920 onwards, a small organisation of educators formed around Tsunesaburo Makiguchi. Makiguchi was then head teacher of a primary school. Josei Toda, who later became his closest follower, joined the teaching staff. As their relationship deepened, Toda began to look upon Makiguchi, not so much as the head teacher, but as his own lifelong teacher. So it was no surprise that when Makiguchi began to practise Nichiren Shoshu, Toda followed. Soon after, an embryo organisation was formed, mainly among educators and directed towards educational reform. This organisation was the forerunner of the Soka Gakkai. It called itself Soka Kyoiku Gakkai (literally 'value creating education society') and continued to grow until it reached its peak in 1941. As time passed, its motivation and purpose became religious rather than educational.

The militaristic government had imposed Shinto as the national religion and suppressed all else. Religion had been used to mobilise the population for war, reviving the ancient belief that the emperor was descended from a god. As a part of this strategy, the government insisted on the merger of Nichiren Shoshu with other heretical Nichiren sects, and the incorporation of certain Shinto tenets in their teachings and practice. While other religious groups had succumbed to government pressure, Makiguchi and Toda declared that they would reject any merger. The lay society continued to hold meetings and spread the teachings of Nichiren Daishonin exactly as before. This eventually led to the arrest of twenty-one leaders of the lay society. Of these only Toda and Makiguchi maintained faith in Nichiren Daishonin's Buddhism. The others, as a result of harsh treatment by the prison authorities, agreed to stop practising (one of them committing suicide in prison). Makiguchi died of his privations in prison on November 18th 1944, at the age of seventy-three. Toda remained in prison until he was released, not convicted, shortly before the end of the war.

The world into which Toda was released was truly shocking. For the first time he could see with his own eyes the havoc and destruction he had only been able to hear about whilst in prison. Like Makiguchi, he had suffered very badly at the hands of the prison authorities. Along with malnutrition, he had chronic tuberculosis, asthma, heart disease, diabetes, and a rheumatic condition. He had diarrhoea and his sight was failing. It is very hard to believe that this was the same man who was to play such a crucial role in the destiny, of not only Japan, but the entire world.

Reconstruction of the lay organisation, with its precious mission of spreading the teachings of Nichiren Daishonin worldwide, would be a massive task. The war had broken up any kind of communication between former members and, at the point when Toda emerged from prison, there was still no freedom of religion. Yet there was no doubt in Toda's mind that it was his life's purpose to carry on Makiguchi's work and establish such a movement among ordinary people that the teachings of Nichiren Daishonin would never again be in danger of being lost. This powerful inner conviction came from his experience whilst in solitary confinement in Sugamo prison when he came to the realisation that he was a bodhisattva of the earth, and must fulfill his life's purpose as such.

On January 1st 1944, in his prison cell Toda first started to study a battered copy of the *Lotus Sutra*. Chanting Nam-myoho-renge-kyo ten thousand times a day, he began reading it once, twice, then again, so that by early March he was studying it for the fourth time. The opening passages elaborated on the Buddha's enlightenment and these were quite easy to understand. However, he was perplexed by a passage consisting entirely of negatives. He was convinced it described the essence of Buddha's enlightenment and despite all the negatives was something concrete. But what was it? Continuing to chant and study this passage intensely, he suddenly realised its full meaning. The word 'life-force' leapt into Toda's mind. Beyond any doubt he understood that 'the Buddha' is the fundamental power of life-force existing in the depths of each person: the essence of cosmic life-force. At that moment, he knew without a shadow of a doubt the reason for his existence. Amid the ruins of war-torn Japan this one man knew what had to be done to prevent a catastrophe of such magnitude being repeated. What was needed was to construct the foundations of a completely new and peaceful civilisation which would develop far into the coming centuries based on the teachings of Nichiren Daishonin. To the eyes of Toda, the ruins of Tokyo only confirmed the need to set to work. This indomitable spirit enabled him to re-establish his health and business activities with all speed.

A new organisation began to form around Toda and was named Soka Gakkai. Begun by one individual in 1945, by 1958 it had grown to a nationwide membership of over 750,000 households. The story of this dramatic growth has been told in detail in the *Human Revolution* written by Daisaku Ikeda. There can be no doubt that by the late fifties, Nichiren Daishonin's Buddhism had become firmly established in Japan.

Following the death of Mr Toda on 2nd April 1958, Daisaku Ikeda became the third president of the Soka Gakkai. The two had met some thirteen years earlier when, as a young man of nineteen, Ikeda had attended his first discussion meeting. Toda had been present at that meeting and had had a profound influence on the young man. Since those days, the Soka Gakkai has grown to its present membership of over ten million families in Japan, and continues to grow in a steady fashion;

In the early sixties, Daisaku Ikeda began to travel extensively outside Japan to help and guide the very first people with the Gohonzon who had arrived in many countries of Europe, America, Latin America and Asia. During the last twenty years Nichiren Shoshu organisations have begun to grow outside Japan. Now, with the strong establishment of Nichiren Shoshu in Japan and in over 100 other countries of the world, more and more people are becoming aware of Nichiren Daishonin's Buddhism and of the means it provides to control the devilish impulses inherent in human life, which are the source of war and all other evils. In this way a 'peace force' of ordinary people spanning the world is evolving which aims towards the next century being founded on the absolute dignity of life itself. Whether the human race can turn the 21st century into the 'century of life', will depend on the achievement of these bodhisattvas of the earth as we enter the next century.

Working for peace

by Jim Cowan

The deepest dream of each human being is to live fully, without regret and to have created something of value to leave behind. If people around the world were able to live like this, there would hardly be doubt about peace in the world; it would surely be a reality. But it is not and people do not generally live in such a way. Peace in the world and the way of life of the individual are deeply connected and nowhere more so than in practising Buddhism.

One person starts to practice, then another; more follow and soon an organisation comes into being and that simple fact could, at first sight, appear to hamper any real possibility of a world at peace. After all, it frequently happens that the very organisation set up to make an improvement in society, actually becomes a barrier to achieving that goal. Daisaku Ikeda has said this about organisations:

'Together with technology and communications, organisation is a major pillar of our civilisation. As such, it has been a source of blessing for mankind. At the same time, it undeniably poses a grave threat. Society, itself an organisational form created by man, reflects human intentions. But social mechanisms occasionally function in totally undesirable ways. It is one of the tragedies of our times that the autonomous action of organised society sometimes suppresses and even rejects humanity.'[1]

So . . . what kind of organisation comes into being when many people start to practise Buddhism?

Such an organisation is a means for its members to change their lives. To illustrate, a family sharing a house has to struggle to maintain good relations, continue to respect one another, and overcome problems. Likewise, the diverse members of a Nichiren Shoshu organisation who meet regularly, find that the difficulty they have in relating to each other presents a vital opportunity for them to open up their lives and overcome something inside. This is human revolution or the modern way of referring to this deepest of human desires: attaining Buddhahood.

Human revolution, or personal change, because it emanates from the depths of our lives, also creates an effect in society. The flow of Nichiren

Daishonin's teachings into society, either through the natural process of change within individuals or as a result of collective activities, is known as Kosen rufu. Human revolution is the inside change. Kosen rufu is the much wider impact of this in all spheres and aspects of society, the natural environment, and the world itself. So this is the second important point about an organisation of people practising Buddhism: it doesn't mean introspection, it actually affects the real world we all live in. Again, Daisaku Ikeda has expressed this principle with clarity:

> 'There is a widespread misunderstanding that religious faith is only a matter of a human being's inner world, or that a religious person is one who withdraws to some quiet place and devotes himself to contemplation. If this were the case, religion would be too egoistic. As long as faith remains limited to one's inner world, its significance will not be great. It should spread outwards and influence the realities of life and society.... It is precisely because our faith can positively influence the environment that we dedicate ourselves to the cause of Kosen rufu'.[2]

To sum up then, the goals of any Nichiren Shoshu organisation are to enable its members to achieve their individual human revolution and at the same time create value in society.

How does this translate into action? Members of NSUK (Nichiren Shoshu of the United Kingdom) hold regular discussion meetings in districts which are anything from eight to twenty five or more members. As a district's monthly meetings increase in size, new ones are formed. Within a district, there are also small groups where people can get to know each other better and have more time to talk than might be possible in the larger discussion meetings. Districts and groups have leaders who are in no way higher or superior but, in fact, depend completely on the support of their members. Someone who becomes a leader in a Nichiren Shoshu organisation increases his or her personal sphere of responsibility. Furthermore, since activities carried out within the framework of the Gohonzon and Nam-myoho-renge-kyo bring tremendous good fortune, leadership is regarded in a completely different way.

For outsiders to Buddhism, it is extremely difficult to understand how leadership can function on an equal basis and in a very positive way. In society, leadership is often regarded negatively by those supposedly being led. Consequently the abilities of such leaders suffer. The heart of the difference between any Nichiren Shoshu organisation and others in society is that every member has direct access to the Gohonzon. Through their practice to the Gohonzon all difficulties confronting members, whether they be leaders or not, become fuel for individual human revolution. For this reason there is no such thing as deadlock.

Another stumbling block can be the impression, perhaps carried over from experience of being involved in something previously, that by its very nature any organisation represses individuality. Unity is vital amongst members of Nichiren Shoshu organisations both for the achievement of individual human revolution, and the wider goal of Kosen rufu. Mention of this at an early stage of practice can, for some, also be misinterpreted.

In Nichiren Daishonin's Buddhism, true unity is dependent on the expression of individuality. In the broad goal of Kosen rufu, there is limitless scope for unique contributions by many individuals. All individual effort will dovetail and harmonise, through the relationship each person has with the Gohonzon. The result will be far greater than at first seemed possible.

Unity in Buddhism means that individuals displaying their own character and abilities to the full, share the same aim of faith in the Gohonzon and the attainment of Kosen rufu. In his 'Oral Teachings' Nichiren Daishonin said:

'Cherry, plum, peach and damson blossoms all have their own qualities and manifest the three properties of the original Buddha without changing their own character.'[3]

There are actually four kinds of unity or disunity. Fascism can be summed up in the phrase one body, one mind, ie trying to make everyone the same in body and mind. The second kind is many bodies, many minds. Society exhibits this where many different people and groups of people have different aims. The disunity of a body of people who are not united in their goals can be summed up by the phrase one body, many minds. It can also mean a single, indecisive person; ie someone at cross purposes with himself is bound to fail.

Nichiren Daishonin reveals the unity of many bodies, one mind as the basis for the transmission of the Law in 'Heritage of the Ultimate Law of Life':

All disciples and believers of Nichiren should chant Nam-myoho-renge-kyo with one mind, transcending all differences among themselves to become as inseparable as fish and the water in which they swim. This spiritual bond is the basis for the universal transmission of the ultimate Law of life and death. Herein lies the true goal of Nichiren's propagation. When you are so united, even the great hope for Kosen rufu can be fulfilled without fail.'[4]

Transcending differences means overcoming our hatred, narrow-mindedness and arrogance. It means being able to respect each other, work together in harmonious unity, and realise that we reveal our Buddha nature through our relationships with others.

The Law is not abstract but manifests itself in the harmonious unity of many in body, one in mind.

Districts in NSUK currently hold one discussion meeting a month which is open to anyone who wants to come. These meetings provide encouragement: they are where we learn much more about life, where people can challenge their limitations, and where people can hear about experiences of practising Buddhism firsthand and work out what it means for them.

NSUK has also adopted a system of meetings specifically for women, men, young women and young men. The idea is that people of each sex, at different stages of life, have much to discuss which is not relevant to others older, younger or of a different sex. Moreover, each has a distinctive role in the creation of Kosen rufu.

Districts are linked together in chapters which in turn form headquarters (of which there are presently 18 in the UK). Everyone, irrespective of the responsibility they have, is completely equal. The entire organisation has no autonomous existence apart from the lives of the many people who practise to the Gohonzon. In so far as each person can reveal the Gohonzon in his own life, and come to base his thoughts and actions on the highest state in his life, then the entire organisation functions in rhythm, with complete trust between its members. This is the major factor which enables a Nichiren Shoshu organisation to be a vehicle for peace; not the form of the organisation (although it obviously is of importance), but through each individual's relationship with the Gohonzon.

Working in harmony with the chapter and district meetings, NSUK has founded a cultural movement. Members who are teachers, doctors, lawyers, nurses, or who work in the City meet together to discuss the application of the teachings and practice of Nichiren Daishonin's Buddhism to their own fields. Likewise, members in the performing arts, both professional and amateur, from time to time stage musical shows or concerts expressing their hopes for the future and the joy deriving from their Buddhist practice. Members with cultural backgrounds relating to South East Asia, India, Africa, the Caribbean, Eastern Europe and Japan also meet together from time to time. Although normally taking part in activities together with everyone else, this enables them to discuss Buddhism in relationship to their own cultural backgrounds.

But this is not the end of the matter. Nichiren Shoshu organisations contribute to peace in much more conspicuous ways. In the same way that small groups become headquarters, so too, the Nichiren Shoshu organisations in 100 countries throughout the world, together make up the Soka Gakkai International (SGI) whose president, Daisaku Ikeda, has engaged eminent scholars in a series of published dialogues and leading politicians in programmes for cultural and educational exchange. This large scale movement for world peace has been able to present organisations like the United Nations with petitions of fourteen million signatures, deploring the nuclear threat and concrete proposals for the gradual elimination of nuclear weapons. Finally, the

SGI provides ordinary people with an international forum, influencing worldwide bodies.

In his dialogue with Daisaku Ikeda, the late Arnold Toynbee points out that a 'new' religion could never spread and gain acceptance worldwide through any threat or coercion. It would have to be something that people decided to do of their own free will. While any Nichiren Shoshu organisation has a deep commitment to the goals of peace, culture and human freedom, it can only move into these arenas in a conspicuous way in so far as its members are willing and able to do so.

The fact that a Nichiren Shoshu organisation is so different from others in society, is a factor of major importance and yet unfortunate experiences of other organisations means that some people coming into Buddhism do so because they feel that here they do not have to 'belong' to anything. Such people can and do start to chant Nam-myoho-renge-kyo and begin practising without any commitment to many of the things mentioned above. However as they continue to practise and challenge many personal problems and questions, they begin to see the greatness of a Nichiren Shoshu organisation as a new, open and human form of society based on absolute equality and the dignity of life.

In essence, a Nichiren Shoshu organisation is where human beings can realise their deepest dream. It is an arena in which the autonomous actions of individuals actually harmonise, so long as they are based on the Gohonzon. The reason this can happen is that the people who chant Nam-myoho-renge-kyo and practise to the Gohonzon are in rhythm. They share the same basis for all their plans and actions: the fundamental Law of life.

REFERENCES

(1) Arnold Toynbee and Daisaku Ikeda *Choose Life* Oxford University Press 1976, page 126

(2) See later article by Daisaku Ikeda *The True Entity of Life: A Lecture* Originally published in *UK Express* No. 122 August 1981, pages 9–12

(3) 'Oral Teachings' *Japanese Collection* page 784

(4) 'Heritage of the Ultimate Law of Life' *Major Writings* Vol. 1, page 23

Peace must prevail for mankind

by Daisaku Ikeda

Goethe once said:
'Altogether, national hatred is something peculiar. You will always find it strongest and most violent where there is the lowest degree of culture. But there is a degree where it vanishes altogether and where a person stands to a certain extent above nations, and feels the weal or woe of a neighbouring people as if it had happened to his own. This degree of culture was comfortable to my nature . . .'
I fully agree with these words. I am convinced that the essence of oriental Buddhism, which is the Buddhism of Nichiren Daishonin, can provide the basis for the establishment of 'a degree . . . where a person . . . feels the weal or woe of a neighbouring people as if it had happened to his own'.

As is evident from the entire history of mankind, there invariably exists some kind of concept, philosophy or religion, to serve as the underpinning for any 'culture' and 'era of peace'. This is comparable to a subterranean water supply; it is unseen but essential. Also, as a tree cannot survive without roots, neither can peace and culture flourish without a foundation.

Still, it may be said of all the world's philosophies, systems of thought and religion that, though they were meant to direct the current of the age, they are no longer capable of controlling basic human nature. In other words, it may be said that man is now unable to suppress his evil desires and has fallen prey to his ego. Such philosophies, concepts and religions are unable to cope with the extreme speed with which the times and people's values change, or with the diversity of change inherent in human culture. As a result, they have become bereft of the power to provide their respective peoples, let alone the entire human race, with a precise direction in life; one that restores vigour and instills courage.

The Buddhism of Nichiren Daishonin is the Buddhism of the sun which illuminates all mankind. The Nichiren Shoshu Buddhist sect, grounded in a tradition of 700 years, expounds the principle of cause and effect, which is a thorough elucidation of a valid and consistent outlook on life and living, on human society, and the universe at large. It is this great Buddhism which embraces the most fundamental basis for the peace of mankind in the 21st century.

People naturally desire peace on this planet above all else. Their dream is for the flowering of human culture in the soil of perpetual peace in this world. It is only natural that people desire to live happily to the end. Man is aware of the cruelty and barbarity of war, but peace can never be attained by waiting for it passively. In order to secure their right to happiness, each and every individual of every nationality must now be awakened to the growing necessity to proclaim their demands for peace.

In any case, neither peace nor culture can be born only of concepts. People must realise that a firm foundation of true peace and culture can be constructed only through action; through the practice of a profound and steadfast faith, or principle, which lays the greatest stress on absolute respect for life. Not publicity or idealism, but action, in its real sense, is required for this cause today.

It was only a decade ago that it was popularly thought that the nuclear powers' arsenal of weapons would be mutually deterrent. The foolish illusion that an enemy nation would not wage war with a nuclear power for fear of reprisal (that nuclear weapons would serve as a brake on war) was adamantly declared at the time. I term this an illusion because this type of reasoning is grounded in and fed by mutual distrust, mutual hatred and simple fear of nuclear weapons; feelings which are actually the very cause for war itself. Sure enough, this idea of the unusability of nuclear weapons was shattered, and now nuclear weapons are rapidly exposing their truly devilish nature. Recent arguments over how to wage a first strike to gain victory obviously imply the framing of strategic programmes, in which nuclear weapons are no longer unusable but usable. The recently introduced neutron bomb is capable of instantaneously annihilating man without devastating buildings, but it may be said that this new weapon is only an extension of the same old argument; an inevitable product of an argument based upon distrust, hatred and fear.

Buddhism elucidates the two basic aspects inherent in human life as fundamental darkness and ultimate enlightenment. Fundamental darkness activates our evil nature and unhappiness in life, while ultimate enlightenment does the same for the power of good and happiness. Buddhism terms the roots of human distrust, hatred and fear as fundamental darkness.

I would like to emphasise that we are now facing an age which requires a revolution of life. This implies that we cannot discuss peace or culture in their true sense if we neglect the necessity for an assiduous practice of faith in the essential teaching of Buddhism. This faith awakens the wisdom within each individual to live in peace and happiness. In other words, I would like to underline that this faith enables the transformation of fundamental darkness into ultimate enlightenment. Consequently, it is an undoubted fact that our movement, rooted in this faith, will continue to increase in significance as we proceed towards the 21st century.

A passage from one of Nichiren Daishonin's writings, the 'Letter from Sado', reads:
'The most dreadful things in the world are the pain of fire, the flashing of swords and the shadow of death'.[1]
This excerpt contains the true aspect of human nature and states that what man dreads most are the pain of fire and the flashing of swords, namely, war in modern terms; as well as the inevitable reality of dying. Nichiren Daishonin's Buddhism is absolutely against war and it thoroughly clarifies the issue of life and death; thereby enabling man to accept his fate positively and with composure.

It may be said that all leaders, all races and all the organisations of the world are presently sharing an unavoidable destiny; that there is no alternative for man but, with wisdom, effort and patience, to reject war absolutely. If we shirk this single task, no endeavour, no argument, in fact nothing will be effective, for all will eventually be reduced to ashes.

REFERENCE

(1) 'Letter from Sado' *Major Writings* Vol 1, page 33

Part 4.
In Conclusion

Faith, practice and study

'How to practise as the Buddha taught?'. This final part answers the crucial question by explaining the three ways of faith, practice and study.

The key to attaining Buddhahood is faith. What does this word mean in Buddhism? The Chinese character *shin* is itself composed of two characters meaning 'person' and 'words, speak'. It literally means 'words the person speaks'. However, the Chinese also implies that faith means 'not to doubt' and 'to speak the truth'. The *Lotus Sutra* was the teaching in which Shakyamuni most stressed the need for faith. In Nichiren Daishonin's Buddhism nothing is more important than strong deep faith; 'Only with faith can one enter Buddhahood'.

Buddhahood cannot be realised through the intellect. Intellectual processes imply a distance between ourselves and the object. Faith works by taking the object into our own lives and grasping it inwardly. However, faith in Buddhism can never be blind. It absolutely depends on greater and greater awareness. Thus 'faith without doubt' does not mean blind faith, because study is an integral aspect of the practice to attain Buddhahood. Doubt is of great value if it spurs a seeking mind to find answers. Without continual study, it becomes impossible to know why one is practising and what one is doing.

Practice in Buddhism is for oneself and others. Practice for oneself and others comprises the daily practice of gongyo, chanting Nam-myoho-renge-kyo to the Gohonzon, and teaching others about the principles of Nichiren Daishonin's Buddhism and how to practise and apply these principles to every aspect of daily life.

However, it is the dynamic inter-relationships between these three elements of faith, practice and study which are the driving force of the practice to attain Buddhahood. Virtually no one starts with strong faith. But through practice and study it arises naturally. Practice and study are like hooks that faith can latch on to. Thus faith manifests itself in action, and action in turn deepens faith.

The true entity of life: A lecture

by Daisaku Ikeda

'Exert yourself in the two ways of practice and study. Without practice and study, there can be no Buddhism. You must not only persevere yourself; you must also teach others. Both practice and study arise from faith. Teach others to the best of your ability, even if only a single sentence or phrase.'[1]
Nichiren Daishonin wrote the letter (of which this is an extract) in May 1273 on the island of Sado and sent it to one of his disciples, Sairen-bo. Sairen-bo was a learned priest who had formerly belonged to the Tendai sect, but he was drawn to the Daishonin's noble character and became his disciple around February 1272. He followed his new teacher's guidance faithfully, and out of his profound desire for understanding, asked the Daishonin to explain some fundamental Buddhist doctrines. In answer, the Daishonin wrote such important letters as 'Heritage of the Ultimate Law of Life', 'The Oral Teachings', and 'On the Attainment of Buddhahood by Insentient Beings'. 'The True Entity of Life' is another of these letters. Its title comes from the phrase *shoho jisso*, or 'the true entity of all phenomena', which appears in the second chapter of the *Lotus Sutra*. Rather than giving a purely literal explanation, the Daishonin clarified the profound meaning of this phrase from the viewpoint of his own enlightenment.

The passage above appears in the concluding section of 'The True Entity of Life' and explains the fundamental path of faith and practice for all followers of Nichiren Daishonin. As Nichiren Shoshu members, we carry out the fundamentals of faith, practice and study just as the Daishonin taught us, while revering the 67th High Priest, Nikken Shonin as the legitimate successor of Nichiren Shoshu Buddhism.

The three elements of faith, practice and study are actually inseparable. In this passage, however, Nichiren Daishonin with great insight draws a distinction between faith on the one hand and practice and study on the other. By so doing, he teaches us to base all our actions, including practice and study, on our faith in the Gohonzon.

I believe that one of his reasons for distinguishing faith from study and practice can be grasped from the sentence preceding the aforementioned passage. It states:
'Believe in the Gohonzon, the supreme object of worship in

the world. Forge strong faith and receive the protection of Shakyamuni, Taho and all the other Buddhas.'[2]

If your faith in the Dai-Gohonzon is strong and profound, you will enjoy the protection of all the Buddhas in the universe. For this reason, it is important to maintain faith wholeheartedly, day by day, month after month, and year after year.

In a similar vein, Nichikan Shonin, the 26th high priest of Nichiren Shoshu, writes in the *Threefold Secret Teaching* that, 'Strong faith in the *Lotus Sutra* is in itself Buddahood.'[3]

Both this quotation and the passage I just cited suggest that the purpose of our constant practice and study is to strengthen our faith in the Dai-Gohonzon. In conclusion, faith is deepened through practice and study, and at the same time, practice and study should be based on faith. We must understand this relationship and bear it in mind.

'Exert yourself in the two ways of practice and study.'

Practice and study are like the two wheels of a cart or the two wings of a bird. Sometimes you may find it very difficult to continue both practice and study, but both are essential aspects of Nichiren Daishonin's Buddhism. As long as we pursue practice and study, we advance steadily towards the individual goal of attaining Buddhahood and the common goal of Kosen rufu. Some people may want to keep faith by themselves. However, it is not easy for someone practising alone to make constant efforts up until the last moment of his life to strengthen his practice and study. This is why we need an organisation in which we encourage each other. Moreover, in order to promote our noble goal of Kosen rufu and foster the unity of many in body, one in mind, we must maintain close communication amongst ourselves.

Nichiren Daishonin's Buddhism is not theoretical but actual. By this I mean that it is found in the three specific elements of faith in the Dai-Gohonzon, the practice of gongyo and shakubuku (see footnote) and the study of the Daishonin's teachings. By developing these three, we show clearly to others the way by which all people can attain true happiness.

Those who practise, but neglect study cannot explain this Buddhism convincingly or lead others to it. They will not only fail to fulfill their responsibility of propagating the great Law but may even cause people to disrespect it.

On the other hand, those who devote themselves to study without practice cannot obtain real benefit. No matter how much they may know about the writings of Nichiren Daishonin, they cannot draw great good fortune from

---

FOOTNOTE *Shakubuku*. Propagation of Buddhism. *Shaku* means to correct one's evil mind or rectify erroneous thoughts. *Buku* signifies leading one to embrace the Law. As practice for others, shakubuku enables one to change bad karma.

the Mystic Law. The ultimate aim of Nichiren Daishonin's Buddhism lies in attaining Buddahood, and for this, practice is indispensable. One who boasts of his knowledge of Buddhism and finds self-satisfaction in the study of abstract theory alone is no longer a Buddhist, much less a follower of Nichiren Daishonin. Many people of this sort neglect practice and make no effort to transmit the Law into society or into the future. They assume a critical attitude towards those who embrace the *Lotus Sutra*, thereby creating bad karma for themselves.

Practice is divided into two: practice for oneself and practice for others. Simply stated, the former means to do gongyo and chant Nam-myoho-renge-kyo; the latter means to do shakubuku and spread faith in the Gohonzon. These are the fundamental disciplines of Nichiren Daishonin's Buddhism. When you read the letters of the Daishonin, you will find that some emphasise practice for oneself while others emphasise practice for others. 'The True Object of Worship' written in April 1273, explains the Gohonzon theoretically, and reveals the path to enlightenment, setting forth the principle that 'embracing the Gohonzon is in itself attaining Buddhahood'. It deals primarily with practice for oneself. However, 'On Practising the Buddha's Teaching', which was written in the following month, urges us to carry out practice for others, that is, shakubuku.

In essence, as the Daishonin clearly declares in 'The Three Great Secret Laws':

'Now in the latter period of the Law, the daimoku (ie Nam-myoho-renge-kyo) which Nichiren chants is different from that of previous ages. Nam-myoho-renge-kyo entails practice both for oneself and others.'[4]

In short, one who courageously devotes himself to practice both for himself and for the benefit of other people, can be said to have strong and correct faith.

Of course, the most fundamental practice is to do gongyo and chant Nam-myoho-renge-kyo to the Dai-Gohonzon of the three great secret Laws which was established for all mankind and is enshrined at the head temple at Taiseki-ji. However, we sometimes find people who self-righteously insist that, because embracing the Gohonzon is in itself attaining Buddhahood, they need not practise shakubuku to lead others to the Gohonzon. I want you to understand that such people lack compassion.

When we feel joy in faith and gratitude for the Dai-Gohonzon's boundless mercy, that joy will be reflected in our daily lives and spread outwards into society. At the same time, we will quite naturally desire to share our joy with others. All sincere efforts based on this desire produce great benefit, serve to deepen our faith and are definitely linked to the spread of Buddhism.

From another viewpoint, we do shakubuku and propagate this teaching because we wish to help people overcome their unhappiness. Fundamentally, people are unhappy because, ignorant of the Dai-Gohonzon which is the enlightenment of Nichiren Daishonin and the essence of all Buddhism, they live trapped in the six lower worlds and cannot overcome the sufferings of birth and death. They do not realise that the storms of the nine worlds are coming and think they are safe, when in reality they base their happiness on relatively transient and superficial things.

There is a widespread misunderstanding that religious faith is only a matter of a human being's inner world, or that a religious person is one who withdraws to some quiet place and devotes himself to contemplation. If this were the case, religion would be too egoistic. As long as faith remains limited to one's inner world, its significance will not be great. It should spread outwards and influence the realities of life and society. This is the meaning of Nichiren Daishonin's 'Rissho Ankoku Ron' (*Major Writings*, Vol. 2, pages 3–51). It is precisely because our faith can positively influence the environment that we dedicate ourselves to the cause of Kosen rufu.

The practice of shakubuku further strengthens the pillar of faith in your heart. Propagating the eternal and universal Law of Nam-myoho-renge-kyo is an action of mercy, justice and conviction. In terms of time, Nam-myoho-renge-kyo is eternal, and in terms of space, it pervades the entire universe. Therefore, our activities to propagate this Law will definitely contribute to lasting world peace and human welfare. In this sense, our Buddhist movement is laying the groundwork for peace and culture at the most fundamental level.

From its inception, Buddhism has always maintained that the abolition of war is both desirable and possible. This is borne out by history. Nichiren Shoshu Soka Gakkai, which has inherited this tradition, is a religious organisation which is absolutely against war.

I hope you will be good citizens or even models for others, in that you obey the laws of your respective countries, exercise common sense, and put into practice Nichiren Daishonin's teaching that all worldly affairs are inseparable from Buddhism. We absolutely condemn any form of violence. We are all friends who embrace the Mystic Law. While we advance towards our shared goal of global peace in unity, we at the same time respect the traditions and customs of our respective countries.

If we self-righteously think that we alone are worthy of respect and despise others, then we are no longer following Nichiren Daishonin's Buddhism. From the day that the Daishonin first chanted Nam-myoho-renge-kyo he committed himself to his lifelong mission; to the achievement of his greatest desire, Kosen rufu.

As his disciples who believe in his teachings, we too devote ourselves to Kosen rufu as well as to the attainment of Buddhahood, with unyielding faith in the Dai-Gohonzon.

Arrogance or conceit is a shame to any Buddhist. No matter how an arrogant person may try to justify himself with seemingly righteous arguments, in the depths of his life he is yielding to fundamental darkness and his inherent devilish nature.

We believe in the Dai-Gohonzon of the high sanctuary of Nichiren Shoshu Buddhism, follow the guidance of the 67th high priest Nikken, and plunge into the midst of the people in order to talk with those who are troubled, those who seek the Law, and those searching for a more meaningful way of life. We have the great mission of introducing the Buddhism of the sun to more and more people and to those countries which do not yet know of it.

'Without practice and study, there can be no Buddhism.'

This is a very strict teaching. Without practice and study, there would be no way to attain Buddhahood. Nichiren Daishonin's Buddhism which implants the seed of Buddhahood in the lives of all people, is the only teaching which can lead one to enlightenment in the latter period of the Law. However, without those who practise and study it, it would soon be lost.

The ultimate entity of this Buddhism is, needless to say, the Dai-Gohonzon of the high sanctuary which has been protected and transmitted by the successive high priests of Nichiren Shoshu. This year (1981) we observe the seven hundredth anniversary of the Daishonin's passing. At this significant time, it is high priest Nikken who has received the heritage of the Law from Nichiren Daishonin through the orthodox lineage of the high priesthood.

When we devote ourselves to the Dai-Gohonzon of the high sanctuary and, based on our faith, do our utmost in 'the two ways of practice and study', then and only then are we fully living up to Nichiren Daishonin's Buddhism and are assured of attaining Buddhahood.

Faith for us means to believe in the Dai-Gohonzon of the high sanctuary. Based on this faith in the Dai-Gohonzon, which is the Mystic Law of the universe in its entirety, we advance in 'the two ways of practice and study'. As long as we do so, the door to 'the place of the ninth consciousness, the unchanging reality which reigns over all life's functions' is open to us.

At the same time, as the powerful life-force of Buddhahood arises from within, we will further advance along the path of practice and study so that we can lead more and more people in the world to the Dai-Gohonzon and fulfill the great desire for Kosen rufu. To work for the purpose of Kosen rufu based on the reciprocal relationship of 'faith' and 'practice and study' may be viewed as our responsibility, our practice, and our deepest desire.

The writings of Nichiren Daishonin are so profound that it is difficult for us to understand them. But you must read them. For if you do not, although you may practise, you do not study, thus acting against the Daishonin's teaching:

'Exert yourself in the two ways of practice and study.'
I sincerely pray that more and more people throughout the world will come to read and base their actions on the writings of the Daishonin, the eternal teachings of Buddhism, rather than the Bible or the writings of Descartes, Kant, Marx or any other religious or philosophical work. If they understand the principles in the writings, then, from the all-encompassing viewpoint of Buddhism, they can use those other works from new perspectives. I cannot help but declare that the writings of Nichiren Daishonin contain the surest principles for attaining lasting peace and answering the needs of all people.

During the second world war, the Soka Gakkai, which is totally opposed to war, was virtually destroyed by the military government. At that time twenty-one top leaders were imprisoned and tortured. One after another, they forsook their faith in the Daishonin's Buddhism. Tsunesaburo Makiguchi, the founder and first president, upheld his faith to the last and died a martyr's death in prison. Josei Toda, the second president (then the general director), held out until shortly before the end of the war when he was released. Amidst the ruins of war-torn Tokyo, he alone began to rebuild the Soka Gakkai.

Mr Toda asked himself, 'Why did so many members discard their faith in the face of persecution, when meeting persecution for the sake of the Law should be an honour?' One explanation that occurred to him was that their faith was still shallow and weak. They had not had a deep understanding of Nichiren Daishonin's teachings.

Studying the writings of Nichiren Daishonin will definitely help you establish the kind of faith that will never yield to any difficulty. When you read, you read with faith. Study therefore is a manifestation of your faith in the Gohonzon. Nothing is more delicate and complex then the human mind. The mind becomes stable and unperturbed by anything as you continue to pray to the Dai-Gohonzon and deepen your faith in it. It is because faith cannot be shaken by any circumstances that we call it faith.

When the powers of our faith and practice activate the powers of the Buddha and the Law embodied in the Dai-Gohonzon, we can defeat any karma, no matter how bad or stubborn it may be. Your strong prayer to, and faith in, the Gohonzon will definitely open the heavy iron door of your karma. This is the function of the Mystic Law.

'You must not only persevere yourself; you must also teach others.'
Faith in Nichiren Daishonin's Buddhism must always be accompanied by practice both for oneself and for others. Faith must manifest itself in practice. Otherwise it cannot be called faith.

In the light of Buddhism, your efforts to help others embrace the Gohonzon, guide them in faith to overcome their problems or encourage them to practice will all return to you in the form of benefit. Because the Mystic Law is all-encompassing, everything you do based on Nichiren Daishonin's Buddhism for the sake of others, will become your own treasure and make you yourself that much more worthy of respect. Thus there is no such thing as wasted effort with faith in the Gohonzon. And of course, there is no sacrifice either. In particular, those who do shakubuku are noble emissaries of the Buddha in the light of the writings of Nichiren Daishonin and the *Lotus Sutra*.

'Both practice and study arise from faith.'

This is an extremely important teaching which we must always keep in mind. The basis of practice and study is faith in the Dai-Gohonzon. It is clearly stated in the writings of the Daishonin and the sutras that to have faith is the basis of Buddhism. Faith, and faith alone, is the driving force of all the fundamental changes we are making in our consciousness, our life condition and our daily lives, and in our efforts to establish global peace.

Practice and study, if they are not based on faith in the Dai-Gohonzon, are meaningless for us. No matter how exhaustively you may read the writings of Nichiren Daishonin, the sutras and their annotations, if you do not dedicate yourself to faith, practice and study based on the Dai-Gohonzon, you cannot attain Buddhahood. Rather, you will fall into the paths of suffering, slander and false views. Nothing could be more fearful.

From my more than thirty years of experience in faith, I can say with certainty that those members who do not base their actions on faith will invariably reach an impasse. Among former members who have forsaken the Gohonzon are many who, although they once practised and studied Nichiren Daishonin's Buddhism, did not do so out of faith. They may have appeared to have strong faith, but in the depths of their hearts they were motivated by the desire for fame, fortune, position or authority. They were weak in the area where strength is most important – faith in the Dai-Gohonzon.

What is faith? This is a crucial question. As I have repeatedly stated, it is to believe in the Dai-Gohonzon and devote yourself to it confidently and courageously, no matter what storms of hardship or criticism may assail you from without, or what bad karma may arise to trouble you from within. If you can persevere in this way, then you can attain Buddhahood. And if you are convinced of this, then you have faith.

It goes without saying that newer members, in most cases, have not yet established their faith, practice and study that strongly. I hope senior members will help them and encourage their development in many ways. Then they will be able to have pride in following the path of the bodhisattvas of the earth and become respected citizens of their country, community and family. At the same time, they will be able to enjoy their lives to the fullest, revealing their true potential. Nichikan Shonin once wrote, 'Even though one's motivation may not be genuine and true, by relating with the true object, he will still obtain great benefit.'[6]

If you believe in the Gohonzon, the true object of worship, and continue to devote yourself to it, you will acquire more and more benefit as time passes, and will eventually attain your human revolution, thus becoming courageous builders of world peace.

Determination in Buddhism means to resolve to attain Buddhahood, or enlightenment. Simply stated, it means faith. 'Who am I?' 'What is my own mission in this life?' 'What is the life within me that lasts forever?' 'How much can I develop my life condition, and what contribution can I make in society?' When one decides to exert himself continuously in Buddhist practice in order to find the answers to such questions, that is itself the determination to attain Buddhahood. Efforts to do so might be called our fundamental practice as human beings.

New members start chanting because they want to solve their problems or to fulfill their desires. However, if you read the Daishonin's writings more deeply, you will understand that this is not the ultimate reason for our faith. Of course, because of the Gohonzon's immense power, we can still enjoy great benefits even though our motives may still be superficial. However in order to fully enjoy the Gohonzon's greatest benefit, it is necessary to arouse a genuine determination to attain Buddhahood, work for Kosen rufu as followers of Nichiren Daishonin, and live up to our mission as those following the way of the bodhisattvas of the earth. This is the ideal of how faith should be. I would also like to make clear that if you pray for Kosen rufu and practice both for yourself and others, all your individual prayers will be answered and you will find full satisfaction in life.

The ultimate meaning of faith is to have no doubts. A passage from 'The Opening of the Eyes' states, 'Although I and my disciples may encounter various difficulties, if we do not harbour doubt in our hearts, we will as a matter of course attain Buddhahood'.[7]

Because we have various difficulties, we can pray and chant Nam-myoho-renge-kyo all the more seriously. By so doing, we can change our negative impulses, delusion or ignorance into enlightenment. Nichiren Daishonin stated, 'As difficulties arise, we should find ourselves in comfort'.[8] In order to establish such a secure life condition, we must do gongyo and chant Nam-myoho-renge-kyo all the more diligently. Earnest faith is necessary to manifest the true aspect of life, which is eternal, happy, independent and pure, and in which the cause and the effect of Buddhahood are simultaneous. With such faith we will feel an overwhelming confidence from the depths of our lives.

'Teach others to the best of your ability, even if only a single sentence or phrase.'

The Daishonin's Buddhism stresses practice and action. Note that he says, 'to the best of your ability' and not 'if you have ability'. We find in his writings such expressions as 'preach according to your ability' and 'propagate according to your ability'. The implication of these phrases is that although people's abilities differ, each should do his utmost to teach the Law of Nam-myoho-renge-kyo within his own circumstances.

The *Lotus Sutra* says that the joy of faith is transmitted to the fiftieth person to hear the Law. That is, after the Buddha's passing, someone hears the *Lotus Sutra* and, rejoicing, tells someone else. This second person also feels joy and speaks to a third person, and eventually the fiftieth person hears the *Lotus Sutra*, still feeling great joy. The sutra explains the greatness of the benefits this last person receives.

What the sutra means is that the fiftieth person, even if he does not teach the Law or practise for others, still receives immense benefit. Therefore the first person who hears the Law and explains it to another, a person who carries out practice both for himself and others, receives benefit which is that much greater.

Whether you are a university professor or an ordinary citizen, no matter how poor you may be at speaking and no matter what you may look like, you can do shakubuku very well, if only you maintain the joy of faith as a proud 'emissary of the Buddha' who embraces the great Law and sincerely prays for the happiness of others.

I truly hope that, embracing the Dai-Gohonzon, you will advance step by step in cheerful and courageous unity with the distant future in mind, and achieve happiness, security, peace, prosperity and a fulfilling life.

REFERENCES

(1) An extract from 'The True Entity of Life' *Major Writings* Vol 1, page 95

(2) As above, page 94

(3) Nichikan Shonin *Rokkan Sho (Montei Hichin Sho)* Vol. 6, page 108

(4) 'The Three Great Secret Laws' *Japanese Collection* page 1022

(5) 'The Real Aspect of the Gohonzon' *Major Writings* Vol. 1, page 213

(6) Nichikan Shonin *Rokkan Sho (Montei Hichin Sho)* Vol. 6, page 4

(7) 'The Opening of the Eyes (II)' *Major Writings* Vol. 2, page 205

(8) 'Oral Teaching' *Japanese Collection* Page 750

A profile of Daisaku Ikeda

Daisaku Ikeda was born in 1928 in Omori, Tokyo. His family were very poor. One of his three older brothers was killed during the war. As the only son left at home he worked to supplement the family income, despite suffering from tuberculosis.

After the war, his passion for books and philosophy led him to attend a Nichiren Shoshu Soka Gakkai discussion meeting. Here he met Josei Toda (later the second president of the Soka Gakkai), who was to influence his entire life.

Today, Daisaku Ikeda is 62 years old. He was until 1979, the third president of Nichiren Shoshu Soka Gakkai. He is now the president of Soka Gakkai International. His achievements since 1947 have been quite incredible.

Since 1960 (when he became the third president), there has been a phenomenal growth in the number of people practising Nichiren Shoshu Buddhism in Japan. It was also his burning desire to see the practice of Nichiren Shoshu transforming suffering into happiness throughout the world. Today there is a membership of over ten million families in Japan and approaching two million people in other countries.

As president of Soka Gakkai he founded Soka university, two junior and two senior high schools, two elementary schools, a kindergarten, the Fuji Art Museum, the Oriental Institute of Academic Research and the Min-on Concert Association. At the same time, the Soka Gakkai has built many culture and community centres throughout Japan. He has written over forty books in Japanese. *The Human Revolution*, *The Living Buddha*, *Choose Life- the Toynbee Ikeda Dialogue* and *Buddhism the First Millenium* are among some of his works that have been translated into English, Dutch, Chinese, Portuguese, Russian and French.

Daisaku Ikeda's overwhelming desire is to halt the nuclear arms race and bring real peace to this world. To this end he has made a number of official proposals to the United Nations as to how nuclear disarmament can actually be achieved. In Japan and throughout the world, he meets with world leaders to develop awareness of the need to work for peace. During his travels he continually guides and encourages those who practice Nichiren Daishonin's Buddhism.

Glossary

Bodhisattva: Life-condition characterised by compassion for others and action to secure their happiness. Also ninth state of life (see article 'Ten States Everyone Experiences'). The most enduring and balanced expression of the state of bodhisattva is to be found in the role and life condition of the bodhisattvas of the earth whose lives are based on the Buddha state, the Gohonzon.

Bodhisattvas of the earth: Reference to innumerable bodhisattvas who appeared in the 15th chapter of the *Lotus Sutra* and pledged to propagate the Mystic Law in the latter period of the Law.

Bon'no: The darkness or negativity inherent in human life and originating from the eighth consciousness. Negative impulses, delusion or ignorance arising from desires.

Dai-Gohonzon: Gohonzon inscribed specifically for all mankind by Nichiren Daishonin on 12th October 1279 bringing to complete fulfilment his life's purpose. The Dai-Gohonzon is especially dedicated to the happiness of all mankind. The Dai-Gohonzon has been the prime point for the attainment of Kosen rufu by Nichiren Shoshu since the death of Nichiren Daishonin in 1282. The Dai-Gohonzon is enshrined in Sho Hondo at Taiseki-ji, at the foot of Mount Fuji, in Japan.

Daishonin: see footnote, 'A Brief Historical Sketch', page 10.

Devils: Not an outside power or spirit but the destructive or negative force inherent in the life of man and all phenomena. Their representation on the Gohonzon means that we can transform our own evil or destructive tendencies into valuable ones.

Gods: Defined in theistic religions as transcendental beings existing apart from man. Buddhist gods, in contrast, are protective, creative forces and functions of life inherent in the life of man and within the universe which are activated by chanting Nam-myoho-renge-kyo.

Gohonzon: Simultaneously the physical manifestation of the Law and the totality of the enlightened life condition of Nichiren Daishonin; transferred by successive high priests of Nichiren Shoshu as the essential object for the attainment of Buddhahood in the latter period of the Law. Physically, the Gohonzon is a paper scroll with many

Chinese and two Sanskrit characters written on it. The Gohonzon enshrined in the temples, the homes of members and various centres of Nichiren Shoshu lay organisations is the basis for all activities to establish Kosen rufu and the achievement of individual happiness.

Gongyo: Daily morning and evening practice. It consists of chanting Nam-myoho-renge-kyo as a primary practice and reciting two chapters of the *Lotus Sutra* (the 2nd and 16th) as a supporting practice.

Kosen rufu: Literally means to teach and spread widely. To secure lasting peace and happiness for all mankind through the propagation of Nichiren Daishonin's Buddhism. A society in which individuals can develop their creativity without limitation; requiring as its foundation the individual effort to reveal the Buddha state; the fundamental power to create value moment by moment.

Latter period of the Law: Also referred to as the latter day or in Japanese as *mappo* (literally, end of Law). Shakyamuni predicted that his teachings would gradually lose their power and that this transition would be in three phases. The first lasted approximately 1,000 years after his death and is referred to as the former day or period of the Law (in Japanese as *shoho*, meaning correct Law). The second phase was the following 1,000 years, known as the middle day or period of the Law (in Japanese as *zoho*, literally meaning imitation Law). In the former period of the Law Shakyamuni's teachings enabled people to attain enlightenment; Shakyamuni can be called the true Buddha for that age. By the middle period of the Law greater emphasis was placed on doctrinal study and theoretical refinement. The numbers of people able to practise declined. Through his *Maka Shikan* and other commentaries on the *Lotus Sutra*, Tien-t'ai is regarded as the true Buddha for that age with the doctrine of three thousands worlds in a single moment of life (*ichinen sanzen* in Japanese). The latter period of the Law started approximately 2,000 years after the death of Shakyamuni. While scholars differ on the exact date, it was clear by the time of Nichiren Daishonin, that Shakyamuni's prediction had been realised. By that time Buddhism had disintegrated into a number of rival sects each contradicting one another. The latter period of the Law gives way to Kosen rufu 'for ten thousand years or more' with the establishment by Nichiren Daishonin of the great pure Law or Mystic Law, superseding the pure Law of Shakyamuni. In this sense, Nichiren Daishonin is correctly referred to as the true Buddha for this age.

Law: Referred to as Law, pure Law, great pure Law, and Mystic Law. Ultimately all refer to Nam-myoho-renge-kyo, the essence of all Buddhist teachings and the ultimate Law of life and the universe (see article on 'The Meaning of Nam-myoho-renge-kyo', page 54). Pure

Law refers to the true teachings of the Buddha. It indicates all of Shakyamuni's teachings (especially the *Lotus Sutra*). Great pure Law is a term to distinguish Nichiren Daishonin's teaching from that of Shakyamuni. Nichiren Daishonin revealed the great pure Law of Nam-myoho-renge-kyo which is also the heart of the essential teaching in the 16th chapter of the *Lotus Sutra*. Mystic Law refers to Nam-myoho-renge-kyo; the eternal cosmic Law underlying and pervading all phenomena in the universe. Nam-myoho-renge-kyo is the true entity of life revealed through the three ways of faith (in the Dai-Gohonzon), practice (for oneself and others), and study (of the writings of Nichiren Daishonin). In the teachings of Nichiren Daishonin, the invocation of Nam-myoho-renge-kyo is the first of the three great secret Laws; all expressing the eternal Mystic Law or life-force of the universe. The other two are the Dai-Gohonzon and the sanctuary in which the Dai-Gohonzon is enshrined (Sho Hondo).

Mahayana Buddhism: See note in 'A Brief Historical Sketch', page 9.

Nichiren Shoshu: Literally Orthodox School of Nichiren's Buddhism. Nikko Shonin received the pure lineage of Nichiren Shoshu direct from Nichiren Daishonin. From that time until now the doctrines, practice and teachings of Nichiren Daishonin have been passed from high priest to high priest for over seven hundred years. Nikken Shonin is the 67th high priest of Nichiren Shoshu at the present time. The primary function of the priesthood in Nichiren Shoshu is to maintain the purity of the Law and ensure that the doctrines, practice and teachings of Nichiren Daishonin are transmitted in complete purity to succeeding generations.

Shakubuku: Propagation of Buddhism; enabling others to share the eternal Law, reveal Buddhahood, and contribute to Kosen rufu. *Shaku* literally means to correct one's evil mind or rectify erroneous thoughts. *Buku* signifies leading one to embrace the Law. Also important as an aspect of the three ways of faith, practice, and study. As 'practice for others', Shakubuku enables one to change bad karma.

Soka Gakkai: The name of the main lay organisation propagating Nichiren Shoshu Buddhism in Japan. Literally it means society for the creation of value. Originally founded in 1930 by Tsunesaburo Makiguchi (the first president) and Josei Toda (then general director) and called Soka Kyoiku Gakkai (value creating education society). Re-established by Josei Toda in 1946 as Soka Gakkai. One of the largest cultural, educational and peace creating organisations in the world.

Three obstacles and four devils: a way of classifying various obstacles to the practice of Nichiren Shoshu Buddhism. Obstacles are generally something or someone standing in the way of one's practice. Devils refer to one's own negativity which may be a barrier to practice. The three obstacles and four devils arise naturally to obstruct the attainment of Buddhahood. Their positive function is to point out our specific weak points: they show us precisely what makes us suffer so that we can overcome them.

Sources

Nine consciousnesses: Originally appeared in the *Nichiren Shoshu Academy* (NSA-America) *Quarterly*. Reprinted in an edited version in *UK Express* No 80, July 1979, pages 11-13 and titled 'Changing Destiny: the Principle of Shukumei Tenkan'.

Cause and effect: This originally appeared as a much longer study article for Nichiren Shoshu members. This shortened version was originally published as 'Buddhist Causality' in the *Seikyo Times* No 216, June 1979, page 6. Also reprinted under the same title in *UK Express* No 82, September 1979, pages 1, 2 and 14.

Transforming the dark side of life: Based on extracts taken from 'The Theory of Karma', Chapter 7 in *Outline of Buddhism* (see Other Books), pages 165-172, by Yasuji Kirimura. The translation of *bon'no* as earthly desires has been replaced throughout by more colloquial English and the introductory paragraph has been added to provide an explanation of *bon'no*.

How people affect their environment: Specially written for this book.

The fusion of reality and wisdom: Originally published as 'The Fusion of Subject and Object' in *UK Express* No 114, December 1980, pages 13-14.

Ten states everyone experiences: Originally appeared as 'Mutual Possession of the Ten Worlds' in *UK Express* No 82, September 1979, pages 11-13.

Revealing Buddhahood: Originally appeared as 'What is Buddhahood?' in *UK Express* No 116, February 1981, pages 13-14.

Three thousand worlds in a moment of life: Specially written for this book.

What happens when we die?: Originally published as 'Life and Death' in *UK Express* No 109, July 1980, pages 3-4.

Pursuit of the great middle way: First printed as 'Towards the Century of Humanity' in the *Seikyo Times*, June 1974, page 25. Re-translated and reprinted as 'Towards the 21st Century' in *A Lasting Peace*, Weatherhill, 1981. This translation is based on both previous English language translations as well as the Japanese original.

'On Attaining Buddhahood': Reprinted from *Major Writings*, Vol. 1, pages 3-5.

The meaning of Nam-myoho-renge-kyo: Originally appeared under the same title in *UK Express* No 131, May 1982, pages 4-5.

The power of Nam-myoho-renge-kyo: An edited version of 'Relationship Between Gohonzon and Ourselves Clarified' in *Seikyo Times* No 241, August 1981, pages 42-45.

The Gohonzon: Life in the Buddha state: Originally appeared as 'The Object of Worship: Gohonzon' in *UK Express* No 131, May 1982, pages 6-7.

The Gohonzon: An in-depth explanation: First reproduced as part of a booklet *European Summer Course* and called 'The Gohonzon', pages 27-33. Published by NSUK, 1980.

On Prayer: Published under the same title in *Seikyo Times* No 200, February 1978, pages 43-45.

Changing karma: Originally published as 'Transforming Effects' in *UK Express* No 127, January 1982, pages 11-12.

Daily practice: Gongyo: Published under the same title in *UK Express* No 131, May 1982, pages 8-9.

Cosmos, religion, culture: A shortened version published under the same title in *Seikyo Times* No 245, December 1981, pages 33-42.

The heritage of the Law: Published under the same title in *UK Express* No 132, June 1982, pages 2-4.

The growth of Nichiren Shoshu Buddhism: Specially written for this book.

Working for peace: Published under the same title in *UK Express* No 130, April 1982, pages 2-3.

Peace must prevail for mankind: An extract from an address by Daisaku Ikeda, originally published as 'Buddhism is the Basis of Peace and Culture' in *Seikyo Times*, No 244, November 1981, pages 12-14. Also reprinted in *UK Express* No 124, October 1981, pages 2-3.

The true entity of life: A lecture: Published under the same title in *Seikyo Times* No 242, September 1981, pages 10-14 and 56. Also reprinted in *UK Express* No 122, August 1981, pages 9-12.

The three poems by Daisaku Ikeda have been taken from *Poems from My Heart, Photographs and Poems*, translated by Burton Watson and published by the Seikyo Press in 1976.

Other books

The books listed below are all available from NSUK. For an up to date list of books and current prices send a stamped addressed envelope to 1 The Green, Richmond, Surrey, TW9 1PL, UK.

Nichiren Shoshu Buddhism: An Introduction, Richard Causton. Rider, 1988
Over 100 pages explain in depth the meaning of Nam-myoho-renge-kyo. Since chanting Nam-myoho-renge-kyo is the very essence of Nichiren Shoshu Buddhism, this book will satisfy anyone who wants to understand what happens when they do this. The other subjects covered are the ten worlds, the Gohonzon, faith, practice and study, and the international movement of Nichiren Shoshu organisations in 100 countries (called Soka Gakkai International). The Buddhism of Nichiren Daishonin is the basis for a substantial peace movement throughout the world, a truly 'global family'. There is a very valuable last chapter to this book which explains how Buddhism views the creation of peace and which also corrects a mistaken view of a writing called Rissho Ankoku Ron by Nichiren Daishonin. This was his thesis presented to the ruler of Japan to explain why disasters and calamities prevailed and how to establish a peaceful and prosperous society. Today this writing has universal relevance.

Buddhism in Action. Daisaku Ikeda. NSIC, 1984, Vols 1 to 4.
These four volumes contain over 130 pieces of guidance given by Daisaku Ikeda to Nichiren Shoshu members around the world between 1980 and 1984. In addition, they contain important lectures on Nichiren Daishonin's writings, speeches to universities, poems, as well as concrete proposals towards nuclear arms reduction and the creation of a warless world.

The Toynbee-Ikeda Dialogue (Hardback) Arnold Toynbee and Daisaku Ikeda. Kodansha International, 1982.
The dialogue deals in a thoughtful yet practical way with the major issues of our time. It is in three parts; personal and social life (180 pages), political and international life (190 pages), and philosophical life (190 pages). There is a wealth of information and wisdom on the very topics which are of concern today. Those who are doubtful that the perspective gained from Buddhism can influence the realities of daily life should read this.

Guidelines of Faith. Satoru Izumi. NSIC, 1980.

This is the most basic, down to earth book about how to practise Buddhism correctly. It is written in simple direct language and is full of good humour and revealing illustrations. It conveys most forcibly the practicalities of the 'human revolution'. The book contains a wealth of guidance on such topics as marriage, bringing up children, ill health etc, all viewed from the standpoint of Nichiren Shoshu Buddhism. Upon reading this book, any problem becomes easier to solve.

The Major Writings of Nichiren Daishonin. Editor/Translator: The Publications Department, NSIC, Vols 1 to 5

These 5 texts contain in their entirety many of the most important letters Nichiren Daishonin wrote to his followers. Each letter has been carefully translated into modern English and with the passage of 700 years their relevance is undiminished. They are as if written to the reader. There is a very helpful introduction to volume one, covering the historical, cultural, and religious background to the times as well as the life of Nichiren Daishonin.

The Human Revolution. Daisaku Ikeda. Weatherhill, 1974. Vols. 1-3.

A 'behind the scenes' story of how Nichiren Shoshu spread throughout Japan after 1945. The formation of the Soka Gakkai (Society for the Creation of Value) is set against the historical events of that time. It shows how just one person's human revolution can set in motion change which deeply affects the lives and hearts of countless people. *The Human Revolution* also contains key principles for movements based on Nichiren Daishonin's Buddhism throughout the world.

A Lasting Peace. Collected Addresses of Daisaku Ikeda. Weatherhill, 1981.

Thirty four short articles on the theme of peace and how mankind can reform the present state of civilisation towards the 21st century.

The following is a list of slightly more specialised books:

Selected lectures on the Gosho. Daisaku Ikeda. Vol. 1, NSIC, 1979.

Lectures on three very important letters written by Nichiren Daishonin to his followers.

Outline of Buddhism. Edited by Yasuji Kirimura, NSIC, 1981.

A scholarly book covering the history of Buddhism, karma, and two major Buddhist principles: 'three thousand worlds in a moment of life' and 'transforming *bon'no* into enlightenment'.

Lectures on the Sutra: Hoben and Juryo Chapters. The Seikyo Times. NSIC, 1978

The meaning of the daily practice of gongyo, section by section.

My Recollections. Daisaku Ikeda. Translated by Robert Epp. World Tribune Press, 1980.
Short writings by Daisaku Ikeda on many of his personal experiences.

The Life of Nichiren Daishonin. Yasuji Kirimura. NSIC, 1980.
A short, readable book on the life of Nichiren Daishonin.

The Living Buddha: An Interpretive Biography. Daisaku Ikeda. Translated by Burton Watson. Weatherhill, 1976.
A portrait of the life and times of Shakyamuni.

Buddhism the First Millennium. Daisaku Ikeda. Translated by Burton Watson. Kodansha International, 1977.
The first 1,000 years in the history of Buddhism from its historical origins in India.

The Flower of Chinese Buddhism. Daisaku Ikeda. Translated by Burton Watson. Weatherhill, 1986.
The second 1,000 years, centred on China, in the history of Buddhism.

Buddhism and the Nichiren Shoshu Tradition. Yasuji Kirimura. NSIC, 1986.
A full and authoritative account of the historical flow of Buddhism from the Lotus Sutra of Shakyamuni right through to the establishment of Nichiren Daishonin's Buddhism and its manifestation today as a world movement towards a warless world.

Treasures of the Heart. Daisaku Ikeda. NSIC, 1982.
Over 30 short essays relating trends in society to one of the many Buddhist parables.